FRESH FOOD FROM SMALL SPACES

FRESH FOOD FROM SMALL SPACES

The Square Inch Gardener's
Guide to Year-Round Growing,
Fermenting, and Sprouting

R.J. RUPPENTHAL

Chelsea Green Publishing Company
White River Junction, Vermont

Project Manager: Emily Foote
Developmental Editor: Ben Watson
Copy Editor: Susan Barnett
Proofreader: Ellen Brownstein
Designer: Peter Holm, Sterling Hill
    Productions

Printed in the United States of America
First printing, September 2008
10 9 8 7 6 5 4 3 2 1   08 09 10 11

The Chelsea Green Publishing Company is committed to preserving ancient forests and natural resources. We elected to print this title on 30% postconsumer recycled paper, processed chlorine-free. As a result, for this printing, we have saved:

18 Trees (40' tall and 6-8" diameter)
6,551 Gallons of Wastewater
13 million BTU's Total Energy
841 Pounds of Solid Waste
1,578 Pounds of Greenhouse Gases

Chelsea Green Publishing made this paper choice because we and our printer, Thomson-Shore, Inc., are members of the Green Press Initiative, a nonprofit program dedicated to supporting authors, publishers, and suppliers in their efforts to reduce their use of fiber obtained from endangered forests. For more information, visit: www.greenpressinitiative.org.

Environmental impact estimates were made using the Environmental Defense Paper Calculator. For more information visit: www.papercalculator.org.

Our Commitment to Green Publishing
Chelsea Green sees publishing as a tool for cultural change and ecological stewardship. We strive to align our book manufacturing practices with our editorial mission and to reduce the impact of our business enterprise on the environment. We print our books and catalogs on chlorine-free recycled paper, using soy-based inks whenever possible. This book may cost slightly more because we use recycled paper, and we hope you'll agree that it's worth it. Chelsea Green is a member of the Green Press Initiative (www.greenpressinitiative.org), a nonprofit coalition of publishers, manufacturers, and authors working to protect the world's endangered forests and conserve natural resources.
    Fresh Food from Small Spaces was printed on 60-lb. Joy White, a 30-percent postconsumer-waste recycled paper supplied by Thomson-Shore.

Library of Congress Cataloging-in-Publication Data

Ruppenthal, R. J.
  Fresh food from small spaces : the square-inch gardener's guide to year-round growing, fermenting, and sprouting / R.J. Ruppenthal.
       p. cm.
  Includes bibliographical references and index.
  ISBN 978-1-60358-028-1
  1. Square foot gardening. 2. Container gardening. 3. Small gardens. I. Title. II. Title: Square-inch gardener's guide to year-round growing, fermenting, and sprouting.
  SB453.R87 2008
  635--dc22

                    2008026557

Chelsea Green Publishing Company
Post Office Box 428
White River Junction, VT 05001
(802) 295–6300
www.chelseagreen.com

TABLE OF CONTENTS

Introduction | vii

1. Creating a Food System for Your Space | 1
2. Deciding What to Grow in Your Garden Space | 5
3. How to Buy or Build Productive Vegetable Containers | 20
4. Using Vertical Space and Reflected Light | 41
5. Starting Transplants and Cycling Your Crops | 49
6. Growing Fruit and Berries in Your Spare Space | 57
7. Sprouting Grains, Beans, Wheatgrass, and Salad Sprouts | 79
8. Making Yogurt, Kefir, and Fermented Foods | 96
9. Cultivating Mushrooms | 111
10. Raising Chickens and Honeybees in the City | 119
11. Making Compost and Partnering with Worms | 132
12. Survival During Resource Shortages | 150
13. Helping to Build a Sustainable Future | 161

Notes | 166
Resources | 172

INTRODUCTION

This book is a practical guide to growing food for city residents with small spaces. It provides you with the knowledge and skills necessary to produce food from your own fresh vegetables and fruits, mushrooms, sprouts, fermented foods, and small livestock. Even if you have no yard and very little free space, you can produce a variety of fresh food. Using the information in this book, I believe that anyone living in a typical city apartment, condominium, townhouse, or single-family home could apply just two or three of the strategies mentioned in this book and grow up to 10 to 20 percent of their own fresh food. This may sound impossible, but it's very achievable by using a combination of traditional methods and innovative, space-saving techniques. At the end of the day, you may even have enough eggs, spinach, blueberries, or gourmet mushrooms to share or trade the excess with neighbors. In short, this book is about using *every square inch* of your available space to create a fresher and more sustainable lifestyle.

I know firsthand of the need for this book, because I have been searching for it for many years. Having lived in small urban apartments and condos, I did not have the luxury of space that most gardening books describe. When I looked for a guide to raising food in the city, all I found were glossy coffee-table books with beautiful pictures of flowers and herbs growing in containers on somebody's porch. A handful of others discussed what to do with a large backyard, but what if you have no backyard? So I turned to rural sustainability guides and organic gardening manuals, I improvised, and I learned from others who were practicing techniques that could be applied in small spaces. I have now practiced, or observed firsthand, each of the food-producing techniques in this book. By trying, failing, and sometimes succeeding, I have learned how to produce a sizeable percentage of my family's own fresh food from a small urban living space. And I decided that others could use this information too, so I *wrote* the book I had been trying to find.

There is another important rationale for this book, at this time. The world is changing quickly and we need to adapt. For the last few generations, our entire economy and way of life, in addition to our food supply, have been built on a steady supply of cheap energy. We have not needed to worry much about where our food comes from or how far we need to drive to work. But in the coming years this foundation of cheap energy is likely to disappear, and our lives will change dramatically as a result. In the words of Kenneth Deffeyes, a former Shell petroleum geologist and current Princeton University professor, "Global oil production will probably reach a peak sometime this decade. After the peak, the world's production of crude will fall, never to rise again. If the predictions are correct, there will be an enormous effect on the world economy."[1] While there is still oil left in the ground, the world's largest oil and gas wells are beginning their natural production declines just as energy demand is greatly increasing from industrializing countries like China and India.[2] Once an oil well's production peaks, it is much more expensive to pump out what remains, not to mention the rapid decline in overall production, which is the situation we face today with the world's biggest oil wells. Everything we buy and use, from clothes to food to electronics to lumber, is made using these fossil fuels for production, manufacturing, shipping, and more. When the price of oil and gas goes up, everything else follows. The increases we have seen so far are only the beginning.

Mainstream companies now understand that cheap oil is disappearing, and that it will cost much more to obtain, refine, and transport the oil that remains. According to an ad from Volvo, "global oil production will probably peak within the decade, and the time of cheap and abundant crude oil will be over." Even Chevron Corporation has put out the word that the world is using much more oil than we are able to discover.[3] Wall Street investment advisor Stephen Leeb, in his book *The Coming Economic Collapse*, explains the problem this way: "The trends in place for the last thirty years show declining returns from oil exploration, peaking or declining oil production everywhere but in a few OPEC nations, and increasing demand for energy."[4]

Unfortunately, our society has not invested properly in alternative sources of energy, so people like you and me will need to bide our time as public and private entities work to find and develop affordable energy solutions from among the candidate sources we know: solar, wind, wave, nuclear, hydrogen, liquid ammonia, algae, liquefied coal, or most likely some combination of these and other possibilities. Unfortunately, we may be waiting for a while, since none of these alternatives is presently capable of meeting our energy needs for transportation, electricity, or industry. To replace our current oil use with any alternate fuel will take at least a decade of infrastructure transitions and development.[5] So it seems likely that we are entering a period of time in which the price of oil, gas, heating oil, and agricultural fertilizers (among other products) will be much higher on a regular basis. Humankind will need to adapt.

Meanwhile, our insatiable demand for energy has led some to consider ethanol as an alternative fuel, giving a new relevance to the large tracts of farmland in the American heartland. Unfortunately, this appears to be more a political than a practical solution to our energy crisis: It takes a lot of water, chemical fertilizer, and energy to grow these crops, while greater demand in poorer countries is accelerating deforestation.[6] As the demand for agricultural fuel stocks such as corn and palm oil is rising worldwide, the available farmland for growing food is decreasing, and food prices will continue to increase.[7] This is happening at the same time as global climate change has begun wreaking havoc with natural growing patterns, causing alternate parts of the world to suffer from prolonged droughts, raging fires, and devastating floods. These climate changes are impacting global agriculture, making food supplies more costly and unpredictable.

All of this is fine and dandy if we can import what we need from someplace else. Unfortunately, as energy costs continue to rise, we won't be able to afford to buy mangos (or even apples) that are shipped for 3,000 miles to our grocery store shelves. Long-distance transportation, as well as modern agricultural practices, will no longer be cost-effective. In order to have nutritious food year-round, we will need to grow our own or obtain it locally. And, at least until local agricultural systems get reestablished, there will be plenty of competition for locally grown food.

In the coming years, our society will need to (re)turn to traditional methods of raising food, rediscovering techniques for sustainable food production that our ancestors practiced up until the last few

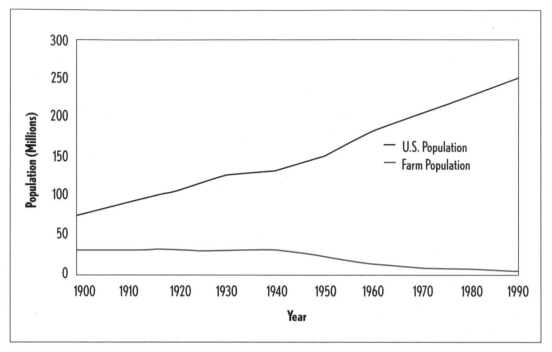

U.S. Population and Farm Population: 1900–1990. Source: U.S. Census Bureau

generations. Family subsistence farming was the norm in Europe and the United States until the industrial revolution accelerated urbanization and mass agriculture. Not everyone was a farmer, but nearly every household had a vegetable patch and a dairy cow, chicken coop, or apple tree in the backyard. You can still see original fruit trees in many suburban areas around the country; most have been chopped down to make space for manicured lawns and concrete sidewalks, but a few of these old homestead trees remain. Some still bear fruit each year without anyone harvesting it, and I have even heard property owners complain about fruit trees because they drop so much "junk" on the ground. You could almost hide a fruit tree in plain sight these days because not many people recognize it as a food source. But not so long ago, our parents or grandparents depended on those trees for their fruit, using it for fresh eating and cooking, pressing it for juice and cider, and preserving it in the form of pies, sauce, and jam.

We will need to relearn basic food production skills in a hurry if we are to survive and thrive in this new world. It is tough to garden when you have no land, but city residents *can* learn to produce more

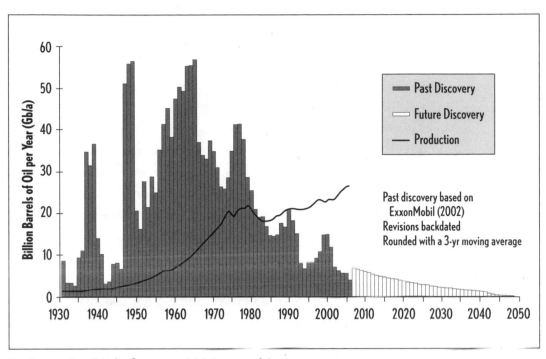

The Growing Gap. Regular Conventional Oil: Discovery & Production. Source: Redrawn from data supplied by Colin J. Campbell

food with less space, and that is why I wrote this book. I believe that humankind's survival depends on our successful adaptation to a more sustainable economy and way of life; sustainability is not possible when we madly poison our farmland with pesticides and chemical fertilizers, scoop up natural resources at a voracious pace until they are gone, and finance every whim with a spiraling pool of debt. Some of us need to start relearning what is real. I believe this book will help you learn some food-raising skills on a small scale, and reap the personal rewards for yourself and your family.

The demand for organic food in the United States has more than doubled in the last few years, pushing retailers such as Wal-Mart, Safeway, and Albertson's to offer organic food to the masses. However, for better or for worse, around 80 percent of us live in cities while only about 2 percent of the U.S. population live or work on farmland.[8] [9] Can city dwellers ever hope to become part of the sustainability equation? I believe that we can and must. My family and I live in an urban area, and for most of my adult life I have had no yard. Yet we have managed to raise a sizeable chunk of our own fresh food from balcony and windowsill vegetable gardens, a kitchen-based sprouting operation, yogurt and kefir fermentation, and a worm composter in the garage, which provides a rich source of fertilizer to feed our plants. Other urban farmers cultivate mushrooms in their garages and raise rabbits or chickens on rooftops and small lawns.

Aside from glossy coffee-table books with colorful pictures of herbs and flowers growing in pots, there are no practical guides out there for urban gardeners who are serious about growing some of their own fresh food. Consequently, many of my urban neighbors do not understand the possibilities. Although numerous books cover rural homesteading and sustainable agriculture, there are no such books for city dwellers. Most rural or suburban gardeners see cities as overdeveloped wastelands with little available space or sunlight for sustainable farming. They assume that serious food production cannot take place in urban areas without energy-intensive systems such as indoor lighting and hydroponics. *Fresh Food from Small Spaces* challenges this conventional wisdom and shows you how to produce a significant portion of your own food right at home. Free space for the city gardener may consist of no more than a cramped patio, balcony, rooftop, windowsill, hanging rafter, dark cabinet, garage, or storage area: No space is too small or too dark to raise food. You will learn how to transform your balcony and windowsill into productive vegetable gardens, your countertops and storage lockers into commercial-quality sprout and mushroom farms, and your outside nooks and crannies into whatever you can imagine, including homes for a small chicken coop, bee colony, or just enough space for a dwarf tree or berry bush that produces a month's worth of fresh fruit for the whole family.

Because I couldn't find a book like this, I had to learn the hard way. Finding little practical guidance on how to raise food in small urban spaces, I have explored, adapted, and improvised. After years of trying and sometimes failing, I now have a productive urban garden of my own. In the small homes where my family and I have lived, we have produced enough food to eat at least some homegrown fresh food 365 days a year. Using intensive container gardening and vertical growing techniques, our balcony and window gardens produce armloads of beans, chard, tomatoes, and fresh herbs in the summer. In cooler seasons we can harvest all the cabbage and peas my family can eat. On a sunny windowsill indoors I start vegetable seedlings, which will eventually be planted into the larger garden. On top of our kitchen refrigerator sits a commercial-quality sprouting operation that grows wheatgrass, soybean, mung bean, lentil, alfalfa, and broccoli sprouts. Every few days, we have enough sprouts to fill our sandwiches, salads, and stir-fries with fresh green sprouts that are rich in protein, vitamins, minerals, dietary fiber, and enzymes (from just pennies' worth of organic seed). On a nearby countertop, we turn plain milk or organic soy milk into delicious homemade yogurt, with complete proteins and beneficial microorganisms to aid digestion and improve the immune system. We get additional protein and probiotics from the other foods we ferment in a nearby cabinet, such as kefir, ginger beer, kimchi, and sauerkraut, which provide healthy quantities of protein; vitamins A, B, and C; minerals; enzymes; and other nutrients for our diet. In our garage, worms eat our compost and produce rich fertilizer that goes back into the garden planters to nourish the vegetable plants. Using our present configuration, we could actually produce enough sprouts, fresh herbs, ginger beer, or bait worms to start a small cottage industry or barter for something else we needed.

I am not alone. I have met others who grow mushrooms in dark cabinets or in a neglected shady spot under an outdoor tree. A chicken coop or honeybee hive can fit on a sidewalk, a patch of lawn, or even a balcony, providing you with a dozen fresh eggs every week or 100 pounds of your own raw honey. Park your car on the street, cover your driveway with soil and straw, and use the space to grow potatoes; you can meet your family's caloric needs for weeks or months on end. Dig up that ugly shrub next to your walkway and put in a dwarf apple tree, fig tree, or raspberry bush. If you have access to a rooftop that can safely support a garden, take some containers up there and plant all the salad greens, carrots, or tomatoes you can eat. Give some to the neighbors. Encourage them to use their own spaces productively, and you can trade or barter for the things you don't have and want yourself.

Using this book, most urban residents can learn to grow as much as 10 to 20 percent of the fresh food their families eat from an average-sized urban condominium or apartment space. Those with a backyard or larger patio can do even better. When times get tough, not everyone will return to the land and become a survivalist hunter or rural homesteader. Yet city dwellers can farm sustainably too on a smaller scale. This will help you survive and thrive in tough times, while also doing your part to help humankind live more sustainably on the earth that we have been given. *Fresh Food from Small Spaces* will empower you with skills you need and lead you to the proper tools and techniques along the way.

one

CREATING A FOOD SYSTEM FOR YOUR SPACE

If you're reading this book, chances are you that you live in a city and don't have a lot of space. You have a small home with an even smaller backyard, a townhouse with a patio, or an apartment with nothing more than a sunny window. Regardless of what kind of space you have available, though—a rooftop, balcony, staircase, garage, storage space, windowsill, or countertop—you can probably utilize it for food growing. We may be limited by the amount of free space we have, but not by our imaginations. This book is about imagining what's possible, about putting those ideas into action, and about producing good, fresh food for yourself and your family, even from tight spaces.

No one can ever be entirely self-sufficient in the city. But in most urban spaces, with enough creativity and dedication, you can grow a sizeable portion of the food your family needs. You may even decide to specialize in one crop, such as chicken eggs, mushrooms, or carrots, leaving you with more than enough to fill your family's requirements for that food and still have enough left over to sell or trade for other things you need. By reading this book, you will learn some ideas and strategies for making productive use of your available space. You will learn what equipment and resources you need to get started. And you will receive my encouragement along the way, because it's important to me that more people start reconnecting with their food sources. Think of this as an enjoyable "mini-course" in urban food production.

As you read this book and learn more about the possibilities, think about which spaces you can use for your food production. If you have space outdoors and want to start a small garden in the ground or in containers, then the most important considerations will be light and warmth. Most gardening experts will tell you not to even think about vegetable growing if you get less than 6 to 8 hours per day of direct sunlight, but in fact you can raise many types of vegetables on much less light than this. It is true that to grow fruiting vegetables such as tomatoes, peppers, potatoes, cucumbers, eggplant, squash, or berries, your space needs to receive at least 4 to 5 hours of strong, direct sunlight per day (preferably more), plus some reflected light and residual warmth. If your light conditions are no better than this minimum, then I would recommend starting with smaller fruiting vegetables such as cherry tomatoes, which need less light energy to ripen than the larger varieties. The same goes for peppers: If you're right on the edge of not having enough light and your summers are warm, you might be able to coax a few banana peppers or chili peppers to ripen, but probably not the larger bell peppers. Bright, warm, south-facing walls can add some reflective light, and a porch or patio light with a compact fluorescent bulb will help too. If your outdoor growing space is light poor, then look to legumes, root vegetables, and leafy greens. Bush beans and peas can handle partial shade, as can carrots, beets, and other root vegetables. Leafy vegetables such as spinach, chard, rhubarb, broccoli, cabbage, and kale can produce even in a shady spot that has some reflected light. Potatoes, herbs, onions, and garlic can function in partial shade also, but they are much more productive with more sunlight. Consider trying a variety of veggies at first to see what works on your site; you may be disappointed by some, but pleasantly rewarded by others.

You also can use outdoor space for growing mushrooms or for a chicken coop or bee colony, giving you a sustainable supply of fresh eggs or honey. Chickens can live in a coop or hutch on a minimal amount of space, whether it be on a lawn, porch, patio, or mounted on the side of a wall. Their manure can fertilize your garden too. Chickens are useful primarily for egg laying, and their eggs are a renewable resource that provides balanced protein and good nutrition. A beehive can take up even less horizontal space than a chicken coop, does not need sunlight, and takes less work than owning a dog. Raising a colony of bees in a medium-sized hive can provide you with 100 to 150 pounds (two or three big buckets) of your own honey each season.[10] If you can't eat it all, remember that local honey is expensive; you can either sell it or trade it (along with extra beeswax) for something else you need.

Indoor space can be used for gardening too if there's a sunny spot on a windowsill or in a room: container vegetables, herbs, and small fruit trees are all possibilities here. The more vexing question is how to use shadier spaces such as extra rooms, closets and cabinets, garages, storage areas, unused bathtubs, and kitchen counters. Perhaps you never thought of these as growing areas, but where there's space, there's growing potential! I have a very vertical sprouting operation on top of my refrigerator that produces 2 to 3 pounds of sprouts per week for eating and wheatgrass for juicing. You could also raise gourmet mushrooms or brew ginger beer, wine, or kefir in that space. Start a worm bin on a balcony or in a garage for composting organic wastes or for fishing bait sales. There are many possibilities for using even shady urban spaces in a productive way.

If horizontal space is limited, don't be afraid to think vertically: I have seen chicken cages mounted on vertical walls outside a person's home, and many small gardeners successfully grow strawberries or tomatoes from baskets that hang from an eave or rafter. A dwarf fruit tree or berry bush can make the best use of a dusty patch of ground or large container, giving you a vertical harvest without using much horizontal space. We will cover a number of strategies to make the best use of available space and light. Think about what you might want to try in your space and then read the chapter on it. Each chapter gives you some idea of the needed facilities and helps you understand how to succeed. I've also included more information on additional resources in each chapter if you decide to actively pursue a particular strategy in greater depth. Since lack of light is the most common limiting factor in city gardening, consider the following brief overview of possibilities, each of which we will cover at greater length in the coming chapters.

FULL SUNLIGHT

This is the easy one: Here you can grow anything you can fit, including fruits, berries, and vegetables of all kinds. Your main limitations are likely to be climate and space, but thankfully you do not have to worry about a lack of light.

LOW LIGHT

Leafy green vegetables, bush beans and peas, and perhaps root vegetables may grow very well in partial shade. If you have at least some direct sun each day, you can try smaller fruiting vegetables, such as cherry tomatoes and banana peppers. You can also try berries if you have the space. In the chapter on fruit and berries, you will find an explanation of several types that may grow well in partial shade. You could also place a chicken coop or beehive here if the space is right.

SHADE

Mushrooms do well in shade, and chicken coops, beehives, and worm bins can handle it also. If the space is indoors, you can use shady areas for raising mushrooms, growing sprouts, or as a place for your chosen fermentation, be it for yogurt, kefir, sauerkraut, kimchi, ginger beer, or other fermented foods.

two

DECIDING WHAT TO GROW IN YOUR GARDEN SPACE

Those of us with limited space are forced to make decisions. How can I use my small space most productively? If I want to put in a small garden, what should I grow? You can experiment by growing a variety of different plants, or you may decide to focus on just one or two items that perform well in your conditions.

There are good arguments for each strategy. Growing a variety of crops is fun, and although it won't provide you with huge amounts of any particular food crop, you'll get some of many. This approach offers more balanced nutrition to complement your overall diet and the likelihood of a rolling harvest (with your plants producing food at different times, not all at once). However, you should also consider the benefits of focusing on a crop or two that grow well in your space.

Why focus? Because some crops will do well in your area, while others will not. You may find it very easy, for example, to grow prodigious quantities of fresh herbs or leafy greens, but not have enough light to grow fruiting vegetables such as tomatoes, peppers, and cucumbers effectively. Or you might decide not to garden at all, and instead perhaps cover your whole available space with a chicken coop. This is fine; specializing has its benefits too. With this focus on just one or two food crops, you may be able to meet all your family's needs for fresh herbs or leafy greens or chicken eggs. And, if you have extra, you might sell or barter the surplus for something else that you can't produce. This is free trade in its simplest, most elegant form.

When I started my first balcony garden, I tried to grow a little bit of everything. In a 10-foot-square area over a two-year period, I grew (or tried to grow) tomatoes, peppers, beans, peas, cabbage, chard, beets, herbs, strawberries, cucumbers, and summer squash. I even had a scraggly little blueberry bush that gave me a few berries in its second summer. Experimenting with different crops was fun, and it helped me learn what grew best in my small space. Through this experience, I learned to focus on certain crops that I could depend on, thus making the best use of my space.

Due to differences in climate and the amount of light and heat that your urban garden area receives, you will be able to grow some crops more effectively than others. Through trial and error, I learned that my little garden could produce prodigious amounts of cherry tomatoes, green beans, peas, and chard. Unfortunately, I also learned that other things did not grow well in my space: strawberries and cucumbers were the worst performers, for various reasons.

Try to grow what your family likes to eat, but also be realistic in terms of the plants' requirements. Peppers, eggplant, and cucumbers are basically subtropical plants that we try to coax into producing fruit in cooler climates. They need a lot of light, warmth, and long days. Squash is much easier to grow, but the plants take up too much space for small-scale container growing; they are great additions to a larger garden if you have a backyard. However, even container gardeners can grow compact varieties of summer squash (zucchini). An added urban challenge for squash, cucumbers, and melons is that they require bees or other insects for pollination of their flowers in order to be fully productive, and it's not a given that your small space will attract the notice of neighborhood bees (though you will, almost inevitably, attract neighborhood pests). Although it is possible to hand-pollinate squash, cucumber, and melons, this requires the extra effort of waking up at dawn and transferring pollen from male to female blossoms with a paintbrush.

If you have the full day's light and warmth that is necessary for squash, cucumber, and melons, and can attract pollinating insects (perhaps with some additional flowering plants or herbs), then you can try to grow them vertically by building a trellis and training their vines upward. Vertical gardening (described at more length in Chapter 4) saves you precious horizontal space and gives your plants the chance to be quite productive. A trellis can be made from wood, wire, string, or even fishing line; the point is to give the plant something to hang on to as it climbs. My balcony has a metal railing that I use as a trellis base for my tomatoes and pole beans; I extend it with string and bamboo poles, and affix the growing plants to this frame using twist-ties from the supermarket or small pieces of string. When plants begin producing heavy fruit, you also need to tie up or somehow support the fruiting branches to keep them from falling.

Some people find strawberries very easy to grow, and I encourage you to try them. Strawberries can be squeezed into very small spaces and even window boxes. A European species, *Fragaria vesca*, commonly called Alpine strawberry, is a hardy perennial and bears continuously from around midsummer to the end of the growing season. It is often advertised as a shade crop and has a truly magnificent flavor. If you enjoy eating strawberries, then they may be worth a try where you live, particularly because of the many different varieties that have been developed in recent years to suit different conditions. In terms of other berries, blueberries can grow in containers and produce well in certain climates, though most require specific soil conditions. You also could investigate blackberries and raspberries, which can be trained vertically to increase production and maximize your use of space. Currants and gooseberries grow well in some northern climates, and can fruit well even in partial shade conditions.

Beans and peas are wonderful additions to the small urban garden. I grow beans in the warm summer and peas in cooler weather. Both plants can produce high-protein shelled beans and peas, or they can be eaten in the young pod stage as a nutritional supervegetable. Both can be grown vertically and in crowded garden conditions, saving you space. Both plants are legumes, so they fix nitrogen in their root systems, making them a great companion plant next to other crops. Beans and peas (especially bush varieties) also can produce quite well in lower light conditions.

VEGETABLES FOR LOW-LIGHT CONDITIONS

For many people living in urban apartments and condos, lack of sunlight is a big issue. Your unit may face away from the sun or get only morning or afternoon exposure. Oftentimes, other buildings surround you and block much of the light. But do not despair; you still have space to work with. The good news is that cities are rarely dark; there is a lot of diffuse sunlight, reflected light off walls and windows, and warmth collected in the concrete and building materials. In the vertical gardening chapter, I cover some strategies for making the most of your light. Here, I'd like to recommend some different vegetable crops for areas with low light.

First, you should know that fruiting vegetables (tomatoes, peppers, eggplant, cucumbers, squash) need plenty of light to set and ripen their fruit. Ideally, we are talking about 6 to 8 hours of full sunlight for these, though, as you will see in the vertical gardening chapter, there are ways to succeed with less light than this. Next among vegetables come those that will flourish in full sunlight, but also can set productive crops with partial sun. These include peas, beans, and root/tuber crops such as beets, turnips, carrots, and even potatoes. I have grown bush peas and bush beans in full shade with only 3 to 4 hours of indirect, reflected light. These plants grew more slowly than their counterparts in the full sun, but they had no trouble setting a crop eventually and the output (though a few weeks later) was nearly as good as that from plants grown in full sun.

If you like to eat peas and beans, they are some of the most rewarding plants to grow, even in partial shade or indirect light. When picked tender and eaten in the pod as green beans or snap peas, both are classified as nutritional supervegetables. Alternately, the same plant also can provide some amazing protein if you let the pods grow to maturity. You can then shell the beans or peas and cook them fresh or dry them for later use. Peas and beans make great complementary crops, as each one grows in a different season: Beans like the warmth of summer, while peas thrive in cooler temperatures and can make a great short-season crop in spring, fall, or even in winter in milder climates.

You will be more successful in low-light conditions if you select the right pea and bean seeds for growing. Do not buy nursery seedlings or use transplants for either one, since they grow far better when direct-seeded. When you buy seeds, you will notice that each variety of pea and bean is labeled as either "pole" or "bush." Pole beans produce heavier crops over a longer period and are ultimately more productive over the same amount of space. So, if you have plenty of sunlight and a nice vertical space, then pole beans and tall-growing varieties of peas might work well for you. However, for low-light or short-season gardens, I recommend bush peas and bush beans. These plants are shorter, stockier, and essentially dwarf versions of the traditional pole beans and peas; they need very little trellising support and can be grown close together for maximum yields. They will produce a single crop (and sometimes a bit more) in short time frame, using less overall light energy than pole beans require. Depending on the variety of bush bean, it is not impossible to have a full crop of delicious green beans or snap peas ready to pick within 35 to 40 days after seeding. These plants also add some nitrogen to the soil, which means that they are a great rotation crop that will help build the soil for your next round of veggies. (This is particularly useful with peas, since they can grow in cooler temperatures.) When choosing seeds, also consider whether you would like to shell them or eat them in the pod, as some varieties are optimal for one or the other use. The best peas for eating in the pod are the sugar snap peas, which have peas surrounded by thick, edible pods, or the flat-podded snow peas so common to Asian cuisines, which can be eaten raw (some are as sweet as candy) or added to a stir-fry for a quick, delicious nutritional boost.

With root and tuber crops, you can do almost as well in low-light conditions, but you will need to experiment. In my opinion, the key to growing these crops is to realize that the beet, carrot, turnip, or potato we eat is actually the plant's way of storing its energy underground. Therefore, the more light energy it receives, the better your chances of getting a nice big, sweet carrot or turnip. Luckily for urban gardeners, the amount of light per day is sometimes less important for these crops than the total amount of light that the plants receive during the entire season they are growing their roots or tubers. So you may be able to get a nearly full crop in partial shade if you wait a little longer to harvest. In fact, full direct sunlight may be too strong for beets and turnips anyway, so a little shade can even help. Also, each of these vegetables can be picked and eaten when small, so a row of plants that never reach their full height may still yield a bountiful crop of petite carrots or beets. For a potato crop grown in partial shade, the plant may only get around

Spuds provide more calories per square inch than any other crop. You can even grow potatoes in marginal soil and climate conditions. ©iStockphoto.com/johnnyscriv

to flowering fairly late in the season, but this is a great time to pick the tender new potatoes that are prized as a gourmet treat.

Finally, leafy greens have lower light requirements than other vegetables because you eat the actual plant and do not need to wait for it to set seeds or fruit. This list includes chard, beet greens, turnip greens, spinach, lettuce, kale, cabbage, arugula/roquette, and other edible greens with similar characteristics. Some of these plants actually will wilt or burn in full sunlight and so they prefer some partial shade or reflected light. You can get a productive crop of delicious, nutritious greens without any direct sunlight, provided you have some indirect, reflected light for a few hours per day. Any of these greens are great plants to use in a small garden because you can choose to harvest them "cut and come again" style (a leaf or two at a time, which the plant will regrow) or else eat the whole plant at once, take it out, and replace it with something else.

One note on leafy greens, including beet greens and turnip greens:

Try growing them almost any time of the year, provided the ground is not frozen. The cost of a handful of seeds is no more than a few pennies, and you will be amazed at the vigor of these plants. Although other books you read may discourage you from trying to plant a new crop in the fall or over a mild winter, many greens are pretty hardy, and can be given a few extra degrees of frost protection by growing them in a cold frame or under a heat-retaining fabric blanket, or "floating row cover." (See "Growing in Cold Climates," below.) At the very least, you may end up with a very short-season crop of baby greens for salad, soup, or stir-fry.

ADDING SMALL FRUITS AND BERRIES TO YOUR GARDEN

Many berry plants and small fruit trees can be raised in container gardens or in small patches of open ground. There are dwarf fruit trees and various kinds of berries that will grow in almost any climate and can be a nice complement to your vegetable garden. Most importantly for many urban gardeners, small fruit trees and berry shrubs can make the best use of your vertical growing space. Please see Chapter 6 for a more in-depth exploration of which types of fruits and berries to consider growing in your space.

COMPANION PLANTS FOR YOUR VEGGIES

Companion plants, many of which fall in the herb and flower categories, add beauty and diversity to a vegetable garden. From a functional perspective, these plants are important in preventing pests and attracting pollinators like bees to your vegetables. For both of these reasons, you need to incorporate some companion plants into your containers or ground-based beds. Most companion plants can be grown in compact form alongside your vegetables. Planting them can increase your garden's productivity through better pollination and pest deterrence.

Some members of the mint family (*Lamiaceae*) serve both purposes, attracting bees and discouraging common pests such as

A rooftop garden in New York City. ©iStockphoto.com/scarletsails

aphids, whiteflies, and cabbage moths. Rosemary, thyme, oregano, and sage are examples of plants that can improve your vegetables' resistance while providing you with some tasty herbal additions to your culinary dishes. Try bee balm and hyssop as well. Nasturtiums, marigolds, tansy, and cosmos add beauty to your garden while discouraging harmful pests. Marigolds deter beetles and some soil-based nematodes.[11] Nasturtium flowers and leaves provide a colorful, peppery accent to any salad and, like marigolds, their aromatic foliage can deter some potential pests.[12] Although nasturtiums are frequently mentioned as a pest deterrent, I have found that black aphids in my garden really like them. This worried me at first until I noticed that all the black aphids gravitated to my nasturtium plants, and they left everything else alone. My nasturtiums were acting as a *trap crop*, and some gardeners plant such crops at a distance away from food crops, though if black aphids do not bother your garden, then nasturtiums would fit well on the edge of containers and tumble gracefully over the edges.[13]

Garlic, onions, leeks, scallions, and chives are wonderful additions to any garden, whether grown for their bulbs or for their green stalks. Also, these plants deter aphids and other harmful insects. Interplanting them with other vegetables may confuse pests or throw them off from the scent of your sweeter-smelling crops. For example, two good companion plants are carrots and leeks: Leeks repel carrot flies, while the smell of carrot plants is strong enough to confuse the onion fly and leek moth, two common pests.[14] However, members of the onion family (*Alliaceae*) should not be planted in the same container or bed with peas or beans, as they tend to stunt these vegetables' growth.[15]

The topic of companion crops is a larger one than can be fully addressed here. Although I have focused on a few useful pest-deterrent plants, there are also many useful planting combinations for vegetables themselves. The most famous of these is the Native American and Mesoamerican "Three Sisters" combination of corn, beans, and squash. Corn is a nitrogen-heavy crop, while beans fix nitrogen in the soil.[16] The stalks of corn, in turn, provide support for the climbing beans, while the squash plants provide a thick groundcover of living mulch, preserving moisture in the soil. These plants also come from different families and have different root structures, so they do not compete heavily with one another for nutrients, and their combination in a garden can throw off potential pests of any one crop. To learn more about which vegetables complement each others' growing habits (as well as the few combinations you should avoid), try doing an Internet search for "companion crops." For more in-depth reading, Louise Riotte's *Carrots Love Tomatoes* provides a nice overview of companion vegetable and fruit plantings.[17] Although some companion plantings have proven themselves over many generations, others are more controversial, and there are ongoing debates within the gardening community about the success of certain combinations. It seems that what works for a gardener in one region and with a particular soil type will not necessarily produce the same success elsewhere. If you are interested in this subject, research it, learn what you can, and try some combination plantings that have been recommended by others to see what gives you the most success.

GROWING IN COLD CLIMATES

Though I live in Northern California, I spent several years in Wisconsin, where I attempted to grow greens and fresh herbs in a small apartment. Our apartment was so dark that my wife and I joked about putting a leash on our plants and taking them along with us to a nearby park to enjoy the sun, just as other people might bring their children or dogs. Though my gloomy apartment was a little unusual as a food-producing area, the main challenges with a colder climate are: (1) a compressed growing season, and (2) a big chunk of the year during which the ground is frozen and very little, if anything, can grow outdoors. This is the reality for a large number of gardeners who live in northern climates.

The good news is that there are solutions for both issues. First, if your growing season is a short one, then choose so-called "short-season" vegetable varieties, which are adapted to produce more quickly. Nurseries in your area should sell appropriate seeds, and you also can search online for varieties that are well adapted to mature quickly. One way to determine this is to read the back panel of seed packets where

Winter greens protected by cloches, aka solar bells. ©iStockphoto.com/BrettCharlton

they list the estimated time from planting or transplanting to harvest. Some types of carrots, for example, may produce a full crop in 68 days, while others can take closer to 90 days to mature.

Second, an advantage of having a small space is that you usually can enhance your whole garden at a minimal cost. If you can afford to spend some money to extend your growing season by a couple of extra months, then you might consider adding a small-scale greenhouse, cold frame, or row cover tunnel to your growing space. There are backyard gardeners even in frigid New England who manage to produce greens all winter long using cold frames and unheated greenhouses.[18] A cold frame is essentially a box with glass or clear plastic on top that allows your plants to stay warmer and still receive plenty of light. Cold frames and small hobby greenhouses (even ones that are small enough to fit on a porch or balcony) cost as little as $100 online, or you can build your own using readily available materials for much less. A simple grow-frame or row cover tunnel can even be built from a few lengths

Storm door inserts being used as a makeshift cold frame atop a plastic raised bed kit from Gardener's Company. Courtesy Seth Vidal. [cc] BY-SA

Front: Juliana double coldframe from a kit (acquired by the photographer second hand through Craig's List). Back: flexible tubing hoops support Reemay row covers. The raised beds are a kit from Naturalyards. Courtesy Linda Nellett.

of wood, wire for a frame, and some clear plastic sheeting to go over it. Also, your balcony, windowsill, or ledge actually may receive some heat from your building, and so plants grown in these areas may enjoy temperatures a few degrees warmer than the ambient air, even without extra protection.

Eliot Coleman, a gardener in Maine, grows fresh vegetables all year long in one of the coldest parts of North America. If you live in snowbound parts of the Midwest, Northeast, Mountain West, eastern Canada, or anywhere else where gardening during the winter seems impossible, then he has written a very inspirational book that may change your life. Coleman's *Four-Season Harvest*, besides being a nice organic gardening manual, provides a blueprint for how to grow vegetables in even the coldest weather. Although his guidance is ideal for someone with space for a greenhouse or covered tunnel, it can easily be applied on a smaller scale by urban gardeners. If you have space enough for a container or two, then you have space enough to cover them with a row cover or create a cold frame growing box to provide you with greens long past the regular growing season. *Four-Season Harvest* also features a unique section on indoor growing, which should be of special interest to apartment and condo dwellers. In it, Coleman introduces some truly creative growing methods for forcing root vegetables and second-growth leafy harvests that I have not encountered anywhere else. If you live in a cold climate, this book can help you get through the winter.[19]

Also, no matter where you live, vegetable gardening is not the only option for growing food. Some of the other techniques described later in this book (such as sprouting, yogurt/kefir-making, and even mushroom cultivation) can best be accomplished indoors and will provide you with a great deal of fresh food at any time of the year, whether the ground outside is frozen solid or baking in dry desert heat.

CONTROLLING PESTS AND DISEASES

Plants will be healthy (and more resistant to diseases and pests) if you don't overfertilize or overwater them—the two most common mistakes people make in container gardening. Nevertheless, it is nearly inevitable that you will face one or more serious challenges from pests or diseases. When you do, approach the problem analytically and do not get discouraged. Seek out solutions that will "heal" your little ecosystem rather than introducing toxic chemicals into it. Applying poisonous insecticides or fungicides in a small space that doesn't drain well can cause more harm than good. A better choice, when available, is to find some holistic solution that assists in building the health of your garden. A similar example would be the patient who suffers from a common cold. Rather than inundating the body with antibiotic or antiviral medications, which have other side effects, the patient first should try to get plenty of sleep, take vitamin C, or drink some herbal tea or chicken soup. These holistic remedies are designed to strengthen the body itself and help the immune system fight off the disease naturally.

Similar types of solutions are also best for a container gardener who is facing garden pests or diseases.

My biggest challenge used to be powdery mildew, which would kill off my peas and squash plants around harvest time, until I learned how to grow healthier plants. In humid or maritime climates in particular, fungal and viral plant diseases are always a risk. Possible solutions are to grow mildew-resistant varieties, to give plants plenty of spacing to allow for adequate air circulation, and to use organic controls. In researching powdery mildew and the possible ways to fight it, I learned that giving the plants an organic supplement such as some cornmeal mixed into the soil or diluted kelp extract sprayed onto the leaves could actually help feed beneficial bacteria and make the plant's own defenses stronger against disease. Also, keep an eye out for pests like aphids or worms, and try to eliminate them at first sight, since they can transmit various diseases to a plant quite easily. The good news is that snails, slugs, and soil-based pests are much less of a problem in container gardens than in ground soil.

Some holistic and organic controls for diseases and pests can include a weak solution of neem, garlic, mint, or chili oils sprayed onto the leaves every week or two. Soapy water also gets rid of aphids and whiteflies for a while. Seaweed products and weak vinegar solutions can eliminate whiteflies and spider mites. Feeding beneficial bacteria by mixing a little cornmeal or molasses into the soil also can make the plant healthier, and in some cases these good bacteria will ward off anything else that ails the plant. And then there's milk: A few small-scale gardeners swear by a weak solution of milk or baking soda in water, which, when sprayed onto leaves, is said to have a cure-all effect against some mold and fungal problems. If you don't mind spending the money, your local garden center may carry the SAFER brand of natural fungicides/insecticides or a similar product; these contain natural sulfur or potassium salts to discourage crawling insects and fungal diseases. Be careful to test any of these sprays on a small part of one plant before using them full-strength. They will burn some vegetable crops and may need to be diluted to the point where they are still effective yet tolerable for the plant, perhaps half-strength or so.

Some gardeners report that adding cornmeal or worm castings to the soil, or spraying leaves with cornmeal tea or compost tea, can alleviate many fungal problems. In my experience, each of these does contribute to better overall plant health when used in small doses, and sometimes the benefits are not evident until the following growing season, at which point the problems are no more. Experiment and see what works for your garden. To learn more about natural controls for diseases, either in a container garden or a small yard, I highly recommend two sites with great information and active user forums where people share solutions to common problems: www.dirtdoctor.com and www.gardenweb.com.

three

HOW TO BUY OR BUILD
PRODUCTIVE VEGETABLE CONTAINERS

Ancient peoples believed there were four primary elements in nature: fire, earth, water, and air. In gardening, it helps to remember that your plants need all four elements to grow strong and become productive. First, they need fire, represented by light and warmth. Plants use light for photosynthesis, which is how they create energy for growth. This growth accelerates when warmer temperatures surround the leaves and soil. Second, plants need earth, which basically means fertile soil that can support their roots and provide them with nutrients. Third, water is essential for plants to take up soil-based nutrients and build their tissue through photosynthesis. Cucumbers and melons are nearly 100 percent water by weight, while most fruits and vegetables are around 90 percent water. Fourth, plants need air. Their leaves take carbon dioxide from the air, which, along with light and water, is essential for photosynthesis. Their roots also need access to oxygen for cellular respiration.

It may sound silly, but the secret to a productive food garden is to provide plants with easy access to each element. In the next chapter, you will learn some strategies for getting the most light and warmth from your available space. And since most home gardeners actually water their plants too much, we will assume that access to this element is not usually an issue (though the book's last chapter discusses water shortage concerns). Here, we will cover two other elemental secrets to productive vegetable gardening in the city: providing the best soil and proper flow of air.

Vegetables growing in a well-mulched bed.

THE SECRETS TO GOOD ORGANIC SOIL

Plants have evolved over millions of years to grow in natural soil conditions. In most parts of the world, soil is a combination of rock-based sediments and organic materials that have come from living plant and animal matter. Here, the term "organic" matter (that is, decomposing dead plant matter) should not be confused with "organic" methods of agriculture (i.e., those that use no chemical fertilizers or pesticides). From this soil, plants can find support for their root systems and the mineral nutrients that are essential to life. Once upon a time, all of the world's major growing regions were covered with thick deposits of topsoil that was rich in organic matter and nutrients, including trace minerals. However, with the onset of the industrial revolution and the discovery of petroleum-based fuels, large-scale agriculture became possible, and cheap petroleum allowed societies to grow food crops on land that was drenched in chemical fertilizers. Most farmers today grow their crops using chemical fertilizers that supply only three basic plant nutrients (nitrogen, phosphorus, and potassium). As a result, our food today has very little nutritional value and contains scant amounts of the other minerals that are essential to life (such as calcium, magnesium, and iron, as well as lesser-known elements like iodine and boron). By some accounts, the nutritional value of our food has dropped by 40 percent in the last 20 years alone.

Organic growers have pledged not to use pesticides and other poisons and also have promised not to use chemical fertilizers. In using organic crop nutrients instead, such as composted animal manures and cover crop mulches, organic farming methods are likely to produce food crops with better nutritional value than their chemically fertilized counterparts. Several recent studies have suggested that organic food can have higher nutritional value than conventionally grown food; if you are interested in reading further, there are links to organic study articles available at www.organic-center.org. But if buying organic produce is good, then growing your own food is even better. Sustainable home gardening is the ultimate ticket to healthy nutrition for you and your family.

Your plants are only as nutritious as the soil you provide for them. If you are gardening in a backyard or using a container filled with plain soil from the ground, you will need to improve it for meaningful food production. First, you may want to have your soil tested, though this is an optional step. Using a cheap soil test kit (available at a garden center or online), you can check the soil for its pH acid/alkaline level. A good pH range for growing most vegetables is 6.0 to 6.5, or slightly acidic. For a more comprehensive soil test, including the percentage of organic matter, clay, sand, and various minerals it contains, you can have your soil tested at a laboratory. Your local university's Cooperative Extension office should provide this service, or you can find a commercial lab by typing the keywords "soil testing" on an Internet search engine. Based on the results, you can fine-tune your soil with specific amendments. If you have no backyard, you can either buy some potting soil or mix your own. With most soils, you probably will need to add some organic matter, such as aged compost, and perhaps some natural lime as well. More on this in a moment.

Many garden centers now sell complete planting mixes, which include both soil and fertilizers. I do not recommend using these unless you can find one that does not contain much added fertilizer. If you are a gardening novice, you may not have any experience using fertilizers, so here is a quick overview. The three numbers on the bag of fertilizer or soil mix indicate the percentages of the three main nutrients in this order: nitrogen (N), phosphorus (P), and potassium (K). Without adequate amounts of these three nutrients, a plant cannot grow. Most fertilizers (and certainly all organic ones) contain more than just these three nutrients commonly listed. Calcium, magnesium, sulfur, boron, and other trace minerals are essential in smaller quantities as well. In choosing a fertilizer of the right strength, though, you will need to rely on its N-P-K readings.

In a soil mix used for container gardening, the N-P-K readings should each be below 0.5 percent. The reason is that many of these soil blends are too rich and will actually burn container plants. Also, as you will soon see, I advise against mixing in very much fertilizer; your results will be far better if you fertilize your food crops from the top, and we will cover this topic very soon. Make sure that the fertilizer sources in your growing mix come from natural sources such as manure or seed meal, since their nutrients are released into the soil much more slowly than chemical fertilizers.

Though it used to be more difficult to buy fertilizer-free soil mixes, many garden centers now stock organic soil mixes with minimal quantities of added fertilizer. The makers of MiracleGro, for example, now produce some entirely (chemical-free) organic soil mixes that are widely distributed in a number of garden centers and home improvement stores. Most good nurseries have locally or regionally produced alternatives available. A soil mix contains both organic matter and some sandy grit as well as, in most cases, a small bit of fertilizer from sources such as worm castings, dried poultry waste, steer manure, or bat guano. Common types of roughage and grit are sphagnum peat moss, coconut fiber, shredded redwood or fir bark, rice hulls, vermiculite, greensand, and horticultural sand. For your main soil mix, you'll want to avoid too much fertilizer or else you will burn container plants. Later, you can top the soil with a small amount of organic fertilizer, which will do a much better job of growing productive food plants.

If you are buying and mixing the separate components yourself, then a basic planting mix could include about 2 parts regular potting soil, 1 part coarse sand, and 1 part organic matter ("organic" as in formerly living matter). The best organic matter is compost, because it includes helpful bacteria and micronutrients to make your plants stronger and more disease-resistant. Do not use fresh or unfinished composts, though, as these may contain pathogens that have not yet been destroyed through the natural process of decomposition.

Speaking of compost, home compost bins and tumblers have been all the rage in recent years. If you want to devote some of your precious space to one of these contraptions, I will not try to dissuade you. After all, I devote a later chapter in this book to composting in small spaces, and a worm bin is an essential part of my urban growing system. However, you should know that the compost you produce in your own bin or tumbler will not be a complete fertilizer for your plants. Most homemade compost is fairly nutrient-poor, so you probably will still need to fertilize with a supplemental source of major nutrients. The good news is that homemade compost *will* fill your need for organic matter in the soil as well as providing beneficial microorganisms, so it still has an important role to play. If you decide not to make your own, you can buy bagged compost from most garden centers. Make sure to read the label before you buy: Some compost is made with municipal waste, which can include treated sewage sludge. Although this should be completely free of pathogens and safe to use, it also may contain some heavy metals, which then can become part of your small garden's food chain. I personally would pay more for higher-quality compost made from animal manure, food waste, or even yard trimmings, which should be available at better garden centers.

If you cannot get quality aged compost or aged leaf mold, then use a substance such as peat moss or coir fiber to add roughage to the soil mix. If you can get some worm castings, then these also can be a source of helpful bacteria, micronutrients, and natural growth stimulants. Mix in up to 10 percent worm castings with your soil, then water it right away to keep the castings moist and biologically active. Another beneficial soil amendment that is relatively cheap is cornmeal. If you can find whole cornmeal in the bulk section of your health food store, buy a small bag of it and mix this into your soil to encourage healthy microorganisms. Some agricultural supply stores sell "horticultural cornmeal," which is the same thing, but most store-bought polenta and cornbread flours are not adequate because they are not made with whole-grain corn. Soil guru Howard Garrett, better known as Doctor Dirt, recommends mixing in the equivalent of 1 to 2 pounds of cornmeal per 100 square feet of soil. For most small-space gardeners, a couple of handfuls will cost at most a few dollars, and this soil amendment will go a long way toward helping to establish beneficial bacteria that can ward off fungal and other soil-borne diseases. (For more information, refer to www.dirtdoctor.com.) Finally, don't forget the coffee! Used coffee grounds make a great soil amendment. Sprinkling them around the edges of your growing areas also may help to deter slugs and snails.

This formula will give you a good basic soil mix, but it will have very little nutrient value. You still will need to fertilize the plants from above. Because container plants (especially self-watering ones) do not drain very effectively, watering the soil will not leach out the fertilizer salts the same way as rain does in natural soil. So fertilizing from above is the only way to really ensure that the plant does not get burned from too much good stuff; organic fertilizers will break down more slowly, and the plant roots will take only what they need in terms of nutrition from the top of the soil. In a self-watering container system, this method also grows plants with a two-level root system: The bottom level goes down to seek out moisture, while the top set of roots takes up only the fertilizer they need to grow strong and produce nutritious food for us.

To grow vegetables, I use a fertilizer with an N-P-K rating no higher than 4-4-2. That ratio is about right for most container-grown veggies. Although some backyard gardeners use fertilizers as strong as 10-10-10, you cannot get away with this if you are raising a container-based garden. More than 5 percent of any mineral can burn container plants. Start on the low side; you can always supplement with more fertilizer later on, but it is more difficult to remove excess fertilizer from your growing system (unless you overwater).

However, if you plan to grow primarily one type of crop, then keep in mind that leafy greens such as spinach need a lot of nitrogen, root crops such as turnips use up more phosphorus, and fruiting veggies such as tomatoes require extra potassium around the flowering and fruiting stages. Do not buy chemical fertilizers, which will harm the soil health and decrease the plants' nutritional value for you. Good-quality organic fertilizers (of single nutrients or mixes) for vegetables are available from many garden centers or online, and one advantage of gardening in a small space is that a little fertilizer goes a long way. If you want to mix your own fertilizer, then cottonseed meal plus a little dolomite lime yields a pretty good blend that includes calcium; you also can achieve a good nutrient balance with a combination of kelp and fish fertilizers. For perspective, chicken manure has an N-P-K rating of about 4-3-3, cottonseed meal is about 6-4-1, fish fertilizer is about 2-4-2, and aged cow manure is about 0.6-0.3-0.4. If you are mixing your own, you also should add some sources of trace minerals, because plants do need smaller amounts of calcium, magnesium, sulfur, boron, iodine, and other minerals. The best source of these trace minerals is kelp meal (dried seaweed) or liquid kelp/seaweed extract, though some seabird guano and rock dust can contain a good range of minerals as well. Kelp products are expensive, but worthwhile: Your plants will get a dependable range of trace minerals, along with the natural growth-boosting and pest-busting components that are present in kelp.

Air is the more forgotten element for vegetable gardening. Although there is plenty of CO_2 in the air for plants to soak up, their roots also require oxygen to breathe, just as we do. One reason to include organic material such as compost in a soil mix is to provide a loose medium so there is oxygen flow where the roots can get it. For many home gardeners, a big danger is overwatering, which not only causes more diseases but also cuts off the air to a plant's root system. And in many container gardens, plants outgrow their pots and become root-bound, which also means they are not getting enough oxygen for effective growth. Luckily, you can avoid these problems by reading on. The ideal soil contains about 25 percent air and 25 percent water.

THE CASE FOR SELF-WATERING PLANTERS

The strawberry pot is one of the most aesthetically beautiful planters available for urban gardeners. These curvaceous containers fill urban space very efficiently, since they can either sit in the corner of a balcony or hang from the eaves outside a window. Unfortunately, they also epitomize what is wrong with most of the container planters on the market. If you have ever used a strawberry pot, you will know that it is impossible to grow productive strawberries from these containers, and that even smaller food plants like herbs will be very limited in size. All those little planting holes give the container an attractive appearance, but those little plants in the little holes do not have room enough to grow. Their roots become so quickly entangled that water does not reach all of them, and there is little growth potential for the plant's foliage.

Some years ago, an enterprising gardener came up with a good solution for the watering problems in strawberry pots: Take a short length of plastic pipe, drill some holes in the sides, and bury this in the soil vertically down the center of the pot, surrounding it with soil. This watering tube would deliver more moisture to the lower plants' roots, enabling deeper watering with less water. Perhaps without thinking about it, this enterprising gardener also found a way to deliver more air to the plants' roots through the vertical feeding tube. This watering tube idea worked so well that the plans were printed in a number of gardening magazines and shared among urban gardeners around the world. This may have signaled the beginning of the so-called "self-watering" planter.

Unfortunately, most strawberry pots are way too small for productive vegetable gardening. You might get a handful of strawberries, chives, or baby lettuce leaves out of a strawberry pot, but you will not make much of a dent in your family's produce needs. Productive container gardening requires that you use larger planters. Fortunately, the concept of the self-watering container has continued to spread, and several gardening companies have refined the concept into a much more productive and modern form.

Although you can use any type of container for planting vegetables, I highly recommend that you use one of these modern self-watering containers to maximize your small garden's production and simplify its care. These containers are constructed so that there is a water reservoir below the regular pot space, and the plant is able to soak up the water from below through a soil wick. The design mimics nature, where plants are forced to grow their roots downward toward the water table, and it makes for very healthy plants. If you fertilize the top of the soil only, plants will grow a bi-level root system to get only the fertilization and water they need. This makes for incredibly happy vegetable plants that will outproduce those grown in other containers and often will outproduce plants grown in the ground. Self-watering containers also have the potential to solve any problems related to lack of oxygen and overwatering. Plant roots get plenty of oxygen, because there is usually a space between the soil and the water reservoir, providing very healthy airflow. And, by their very design, self-watering containers eliminate the problem of overwatering; the soil only soaks up as much water through capillary action as the plant can drink. It is often possible to add enough water for several days at a time, allowing you to take a short trip away from home without having to rely on a friend or neighbor to water your plants.

It sounds too good to be true, but it's not. The only catch with self-watering containers is that most of the ones you can buy at your local garden center are still too small for productive vegetable growing. For example, the only type of self-watering container that my local garden center stocks is a round, 12-inch-diameter plastic pot with a tapered base. These are built for flowers or herbs, but not vegetables. Just try growing a tomato or squash in one of them. (I have.) For one thing, round pots are not very space-efficient. Even worse, they don't hold enough soil for a mature root system. In several of these round pots, I attempted to grow compact tomatoes and zucchini squash, which were severely stunted due to the inability of their roots to spread. These plants did produce a few fruit, but in the same amount of horizontal balcony space, I could have grown just one plant in a deeper square or rectangular container and achieved at least five times the vegetable production. The same is true for the shallow self-watering window boxes that are sold by seed catalogs and Internet garden supply stores; they may be nice for growing a few flowers, but even a strawberry or tumbling tomato vine would be limited by the shallow depth.

There are two possible solutions: buying a bigger pot or making a one yourself. If you can afford to buy, there is a commercial product available called the Earthbox, which is perfect for growing most varieties of vegetables. Its dimensions are 29"L x 13.5"W x 11.5"H, and it holds about 2 cubic feet of soil. According to the manufacturer, one box can grow either two tomato plants, four cucumbers, six cabbages, eight lettuces, ten spinaches, or other varieties and combinations. The trouble is that it costs more than $50 for one unit, a prohibitive price for many small-scale growers. If you can afford this, then buy as many Earthboxes as you can fit on your porch, balcony, driveway, patio, or other sunny space; this will provide a nearly trouble-free growing system that achieves truly exceptional results with most vegetables. You can order these at www.earthbox.com and the Web site also has a nice diagram of the Earthbox design and components. Gardener's Supply Company at www.gardeners.com sells a similar-sized Self-Watering Planter with fewer features for around $35. Others I have seen are too small for serious vegetable growing.

MAKING YOUR OWN SELF-WATERING GROWING CONTAINER

If you are on a bootstrap budget, you can make a self-watering growing container yourself. I have made several of my own, using Rubbermaid or Sterilite storage containers, that grew some mighty fine vegetables. If you have a couple of extra 5-gallon plastic buckets, or a metal or plastic washtub, you could modify any of these as well. All you need is the container plus a few materials, which can be purchased for around $10 at your local hardware store or garden center. If you are buying a container, then the darker plastic colors are best because they hold in the heat well (unless too much heat is a problem in your climate, in which case you should go with white). Most hardware stores, drugstores, or home centers stock some of the large, featureless plastic basins or storage containers that work best for this project.

The basic design of self-watering containers is that they have a water reservoir below the growing chamber. These two chambers are separated by a rack of some sort, which holds most of the soil above the

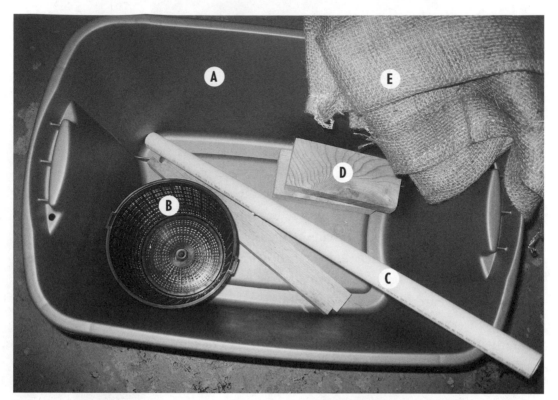

Raw materials for making a self-watering planter box for vegetables: (A) large plastic storage bin (lid not pictured), (B) pond basket, snack tray, or strainer for "soil foot," (C) plastic watering pipe, (D) wood blocks or other attachable supports, (E) burlap, mesh, or landscape fabric to screen watering pipe. Also needed: staples or screws.

water. This separating rack can be made from the top of a Rubbermaid or Sterilite container box that is cut to fit inside, or else you could use two containers, drill holes in the bottom of one, and nest that inside the other. The water reservoir does not need to be as tall as the growing chamber, perhaps one-fourth to one-third as tall. You then need to put a larger hole or two in this rack for one or more "soil feet," which will sit in the water, holding a small amount of soil that wicks up the moisture into the main soil and toward the plant's roots. To hold the "soil feet" in the water, a basket of some sort can be inserted there and then packed with soil for each of the soil "feet." A snack tray or pond basket can do the trick, or you could even use an old coffee can, plastic nursery pot, or 2-liter soda bottle base that is cut to fit and then punctured with holes.

Just below the rack's level on the outside of the main container, you

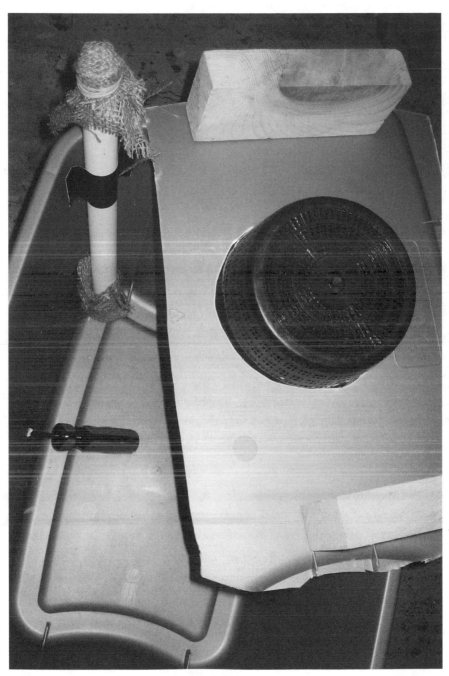

(1) Cut lid to fit inside bottom of container and cut hole in center for pond basket. Also allow space in one corner for watering pipe. (2) Attach wood blocks or other support using screws or staples. (3) Cut plastic pipe to fit height, allowing room for watering once soil is added. A piece of tape will hold it in the corner until soil is added. (4) Here, burlap is used to screen watering pipe from any soil blockage (at bottom) and double wrapped-at top to prevent insects. This "cap" is removed for watering. Landscape fabric or mesh screen also will work.

(5) The cut lid with pond basket is flipped into the bottom of the container, where it rests on supports. The water reservoir will be below while the soil will go on top. The pond basket will hold the "soil foot," which will sit in the water reservoir and wick up moisture into the rest of the soil. Plant roots will grow downward toward the water. (6) Punch a hole or two in the side of the container just above the water reservoir to allow for drainage in case of overwatering or heavy rains.

should drill or puncture a small drainage hole, which allows any excess water to drain out. The final crucial piece, before the soil goes in, is some sort of watering tube that runs down the inside of one corner. Buy a foot or so of plastic pipe or hose at your local hardware store and fix this to a corner with hot glue, twine, or a pipe fastener; make sure that the bottom of the pipe goes all the way down into the reservoir so it cannot get filled with soil; you also could cover the end with a mesh screen or landscape fabric to keep soil out. PVC has gotten a bad name because it can leach chemicals, so if this is a concern you can look for ABS plastic or consider investing a few more dollars for a pipe made of copper, aluminum, steel, silicon, or even bamboo (and, if this is a concern to you, then you also should start with a non-PVC container for the planter itself). The pipe should be wide enough so that you can water it easily with your watering can.

(7) Fill pond basket with soil, pack it in tightly, and wet it down. (8) Fill remainder of container with good potting soil that is rich in organic matter. (9) Plant veggies and water well from the top. (This container shows onions and an oregano cutting.) (10) After the soil has been wetted down once, you can start watering via the pipe. (11) Add organic fertilizer to the top of the soil, and scratch it into the first few inches with a trowel. Plants will grow side roots to take this nutrition as they need it, while taproots will go down toward the water, making for very strong and happy plants. (12) Cover with mulch as desired to retain moisture and heat. If using plastic mulch, cover with plastic first and cut holes for plants or seeds.

When you're ready to fill the container, first pack the "soil foot" (or feet) with soil, wet this until moist, and then put in the remainder of your soil mix on top of this level so it is held in place by the rack. Water the soil from above until it's the consistency of a wrung-out sponge. Repeat this for three or four days, and then begin filling it via the water reservoir. The very top of the soil may dry out, but what's really important is that there is lightly moist soil about 5 or 6 inches down. You can keep adding water right up until it starts spilling out of the drainage hole, meaning that it has reached full capacity at the height of the soil rack.

Next, you should decide whether to mulch. Spreading some mulch on top of the soil preserves moisture and keeps the plants a bit warmer. If you decide to use black plastic sheeting as mulch, then first do the

Vegetables growing on a balcony in self-watering planters.

fertilizing as described below. Then cover with plastic mulch, which can be duct-taped to the sides or held down with the cutout frame of your container's top if there is one. Cut an "x" in the black plastic wherever you want to put a plant. Whether or not you have mulched with black plastic, go ahead and plant your veggies next. Give each plant adequate root spacing according to the recommendations for that type of seed or transplant. Once they are planted, if you have not yet fertilized, then side-dress the plants with a line or two of fertilizer along the top of the soil. Try to place this band a few inches from the plant stems, which will encourage better root growth. For most organic fertilizer, 2 to 3 cups per 2 cubic feet of soil is enough. (This is the Earthbox capacity.) Finally, if you have not used black plastic, then you could now add any other kind of mulch: sawdust, grass clippings, leaves, etc. After the growing season, take out the old plants and try to remove the worst of their roots. Then scrape off any remaining fertilizer (or the first

Greens growing in a self-watering planter. ©iStockphoto.com/CarolinaSmith

two inches of soil), top off with new soil mix, and then add your new plants and a fertilizer band as before. Every day or two, add water into the pipe or tube until the reservoir is topped off. You should be all set!

One caveat with self-watering planters: The size of the "soil foot" that sits in the water determines how wet your soil will be. If the soil foot is relatively wide (covering more than about 20 percent, horizontally, of the bottom area of the container), your soil will be quite moist. If you want to grow root or tuber vegetables in this container, such as carrots or potatoes, wetter soil can mean more disease problems, so you may need to use a narrower item for the soil foot to sit in. Root crops may also taste better if they are forced to grow downward toward the water. Here are three possible solutions to keep your soil a bit drier, any one of which should help:

1. When you are making the self-watering box, limit the size of the soil foot, so that it covers no more than about 10 to

15 percent of the base. This will allow less water up into the soil and allow for healthy root crops.

2. Add a little more sand to your soil, which should limit the wicking action of its organic material.

3. Allow the water in the reservoir to be completely used up before watering again, and do not give it more than one day's worth of water at a time. Advocates of a wet-dry growing cycle also can follow this suggestion, though in my experience, a self-watering container will grow healthy vegetables of all kinds without any special care.

MAKING A SELF-WATERING BUCKET PLANTER

You also can make self-watering planters out of many other types of containers. With the vast majority of large containers that you can adapt to planters, you will need to remember that they need to drain somehow. For example, a 5-gallon plastic bucket or metal pail may be just large enough to grow a single tomato or squash plant, or a handful of strawberry or spinach plants. These buckets do not come with holes near the bottom, so you will need to drill at least one hole for proper drainage. Many of the clay pots sold in garden centers do not have drainage holes either, so vegetables grown in these either die of root rot (with heavy watering and wet soil at the bottom) or they underproduce due to stress or dehydration (with cautious watering). It is a lot tougher to keep the soil moisture in balance when you use a container that has no self-watering chamber or wicking system.

To make a self-watering planter out of plastic buckets, start with two 5-gallon buckets. This is the standard size for paint buckets or bulk storage, though you should not reuse any bucket for food growing if it has earlier contained a chemical-based substance. Make sure that the two buckets are stackable so that one fits snugly inside the other. Ten-gallon, or any other size buckets, should work just as well.

When the buckets fit together, there will probably be a small space in the bottom between them, since the top bucket will not slide all the way into the bottom one. This space may be big enough for your water reservoir, or you may want one a little bigger, which can be accomplished by putting in a few small wood blocks or stones that raise the level of the top bucket another inch or two. You will then want to drill a drainage overflow hole in the outer bucket for the water, and you can locate this just above the top level of the water reservoir.

Since the inner bucket acts as the soil chamber, you will need only two more steps: (1) the soil foot/water wick, and (2) the watering tube. For the soil foot that will wick up the water, you can improvise again with whatever suitable item you can find; this could be a strong snack tray, pond basket, small plastic pot, or plastic food container. If you use a solid container, then you would need to drill some holes in each side to allow water to get into the soil that rests in this foot. Once you have a suitable soil foot, then place it on the bottom of the inner bucket and outline the shape with a marking pen. Then use a strong knife or saw to cut this shape out of the inner bucket's bottom, place the foot holder into it, and fasten/glue/tape as needed to hold it in place (bear in mind that this part will be wet, so any glue or tape would need to hold up under wet conditions). Second, you should find a length of plastic pipe or tubing to use as the watering tube (again, a little taller than the bucket itself), and then cut another hole in the inner bucket's base to accommodate this watering tube. The tube can be attached to the side of the bucket using a hot glue gun, stapler, or bolt and drill. As with the larger self-watering planter, the soil goes in the top chamber and the water in the bottom. As you add the soil, make sure to pack it tightly into the soil foot before filling the whole bucket with soil, as the tight soil foot will wick up the water most effectively. Plant your seeds or seedlings in the bucket and mulch the top as needed with leaves, straw, wood chips, or similar covering. Remember that the soil will dry out more quickly if not mulched, requiring more frequent watering. You could also cover the top with black plastic, in which case you would put down the plastic first, secure it to the rim with a rubber band, wire, or twine, and then cut spaces for your seeds or seedlings to fit. Another option to secure a plastic covering is to use the bucket's own lid and cut out the entire inside with a knife, so that all you have left is a halo-shaped rim of the lid. Then fit this halo rim onto the bucket to secure the plastic covering. If you want a white bucket to retain more heat, you could paint it black

Carrots are nutritious, easily raised in containers, and can store well in the soil through cold weather if you cover the tops. ©iStockphoto.com/merlinpf

or cover the sides with black plastic as well. (Be sure to let the plants breathe, at least through the drainage hole.)

IMPROVING REGULAR CONTAINERS FOR FOOD GROWING

If you decide not to turn your container into a self-watering planter, but just to water it profusely from above, then at least drill a drainage hole or two near the bottom of one side. This will ensure proper drainage and also allow in a little air for oxygen circulation in the roots. Drainage holes will, however, mean that the soil dries out more quickly, so keep a close eye on the moisture level and make sure the plant gets water all the way down through its roots. The second useful step you could take, even if you are not building a water reservoir and soil tray below, is to insert a watering tube. A length of plastic pipe that is slightly longer than the height of the container, fixed to one of the inside surfaces or surrounded with soil, is perfect for ensuring deeper watering. You may want to drill some holes in this pipe to distribute the water, and you will need to cover these holes (as well as the main hole in the bottom of the pipe) with some mesh screen or landscape fabric to prevent soil from clogging them. Even if you do not decide to craft your own self-watering planter along the lines described earlier, drainage holes and a watering tube will go a long way toward increasing your container garden's food production and decreasing your frustration. Also, I recently became aware of an affordable product from Simple Gardens that consists of a container insert and enables gardeners to create an effective shallow water reservoir (if used for this purpose) in your choice of containers from 8 to 14 inches wide. (Available at www.simplegardens.com.)

Any of these steps also will help prevent overwatering. Overwatering is commonly cited as the #1 cause of death for houseplants. This is probably the case because we have a tendency to tinker, and most people believe that a little extra water will not hurt a plant. Well, if that water can drain off easily or goes into a reservoir from which it is absorbed by the soil only as needed (as with a self-watering planter), then you can water to your heart's content with much less worry. The real bonus of a self-watering planter is that, when you top off the water level, you usually can leave it for a few days to be on its own, and even go out of town for a short vacation. Unless there is a heat wave or extremely dry summer, your container should hold enough water to keep the soil and plants happy while you are gone. During the height of a dry summer, though, when plants are turning much of the water into foliage growth, you may need to water once a day.

Following the advice in this chapter, your growing system will be as productive as any ground-based garden. Pound for pound, I will hold up my yields from self-watering planters against anyone who has grown tomatoes, beans, or chard in the ground. In practice, many urban gardeners still may face additional challenges of low-light areas, low temperatures, and short growing seasons. These we will address in the coming chapters. My goal is for you to be inspired and to learn how to grow as much as possible of your own chosen food crops in whatever space you have available to utilize. This is small-scale urban gardening for everyone, and I believe that anyone can and will succeed using the strategies and ideas described in this book.

four

USING VERTICAL SPACE AND REFLECTED LIGHT

If there's one urban commodity that's almost as precious as land, it's light. Most city yards have high fences, and surrounding buildings can block sunlight as well. If your only available space is a balcony, ledge, or windowsill, then you're probably getting less than the 6 to 8 hours of direct sunlight per day that is recommended for vegetable gardening. Fortunately, there are some tricks you can employ to help maximize the amount of light for your plants.

Basically, there are three main categories of sunlight for plants: full sun, partial sun, and full shade. Full sun is the 6 to 8 hours per day of direct light exposure that few of us get in cities. Partial sun is either direct sun for a shorter period, or dappled sunlight that may come through the leaves of an overhanging tree. (Reflected light might also fall in this category.) Full shade is a basically sunless condition in which vegetables will have a tough time growing. Fruiting vegetables such as tomatoes and cucumbers like plenty of light, although beans and peas can do with a lot less. Root vegetables such as carrots and radishes can be grown in partial sunlight. Leafy vegetables such as chard and spinach can grow steadily with very little light at all.

Onions are a little trickier because most varieties are day-length sensitive; that is, they need as many as 10 to 12 hours of sunlight to set and mature bulbs. One solution simply is to grow scallions (also known as green onions, spring onions, or bunching onions) instead, which are delicious and grow very quickly in short and long seasons. If you want onions to bulb up and mature, though, you will have to experiment with the right variety for your light situation. There are a number of "short day" varieties available from nurseries and seed catalogs, and there are even a few "day-length neutral" varieties that have been developed. Your latitude also has an effect here. Check with your local extension agent or knowledgeable nursery advisor for help in selecting an appropriate type of onion.

This chapter will be useful for any gardener suffering from a light deficit. Using the strategies mentioned here, you may be able to solidly double or triple the amount of light energy your plants get, which can make the difference between a miserable and a bountiful urban harvest. But first, you need to know how much sunlight your garden area receives. Time this, and write down how many hours and minutes of direct sunlight it gets. Is this mostly morning light or afternoon light? Remember that the sun will be several degrees higher in the sky during the summer than in the winter.

VERTICAL GARDENING AND THE THREE T'S

Vertical gardening involves utilizing your vertical growing space to make the best use of light resources. It is also an important consideration for city gardeners who may have more vertical than horizontal space available for growing. Vertical gardening is a general strategy that involves some specific techniques—terracing, trellising, and tumbling—to allow plants more access to lighted space.

The first technique is **terracing.** On a larger agricultural scale, terracing is the practice of building several steps into a sloped hillside. These steps are progressive, with each one higher than the previous step. In many countries, this has been used as a method of farming vertical landscapes and of conserving water in the process. Terraced agriculture was practiced by the Romans, Incas, and other ancient cultures, with the Hanging Gardens of Babylon being a famous urban example. Rice paddies are planted on terraced hillsides throughout much of Southeast Asia, providing some of the most beautiful man-made scenery in the world.

On a smaller urban scale, terracing your plants involves arranging them in steps so that each one gets plenty of light. Many city gardeners have an overhanging roof or a nearby building that blocks the midday sun, although their gardens get a few hours of early or late light. If your best sunlight hours are in the early morning and/or late afternoon, then your sunlight will come mainly from the side. An outer row of plants

Terraced planting in Italy: using every square inch of a hillside. You can use your available light the same way, either by raising up the back rows of plants or by planting taller and thicker vegetables behind shorter or thinner ones, ensuring each row gets adequate sunlight. ©iStockphoto. com/borsheim

will get most of this light energy while any inner rows may be completely blocked by these outer plants. By terracing your plants instead, putting the tallest ones in the back and the shorter ones in the front, you can grow a lot more under these conditions.

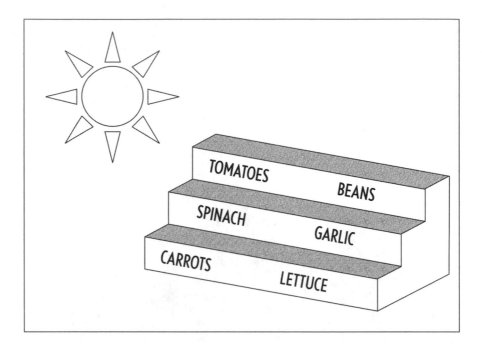

You can terrace plants in one of two ways. The first way is to arrange your garden so that shorter plants such as greens and carrots are on outer rings or rows (facing your late or early sidelight). Taller plants such as tomatoes, peppers, and legumes should be placed further back in this scheme. If you have enough space for more than two parallel rows, then you can either use multiple rows of shorter plants, or else terrace in three heights. If you terrace in three heights, be sure to trim or train the middle row of plants anytime they threaten to block out the back row. The second way to terrace plants is to design the garden itself at layered heights. Using raised beds, containers of different height, or cinderblock boosters, you can lay out the garden so that even plants of similar heights will each get that early or late sun.

Trellising is another great vertical gardening technique. Several varieties of vegetables grow particularly well when trellised. Plants with natural vining tendencies include cucumbers, peas, and beans. These plants have limited root systems and a natural inclination to climb skyward, so they can be planted relatively close together and will make very productive use of available planting space. Tomatoes, squash, and small melons also can be trellised and trained upward.

The cucumber is a great example of a plant you can train vertically. From the moment a cucumber has its first few leaves, it begins to unfurl its tentacles, grabbing hold of the nearest support. It may fix itself to a wire rod, fishing line, bamboo pole, wooden fence, metal railing, or neighboring plant's stem. Using this support, the plant climbs upward and outward, building its vine. In a city garden, you can use any available material to make a trellis for each plant; just keep it less than half an inch in thickness so that the plant can grab hold. A length of fishing line or twine that is tightly wrapped back and forth from a railing or nearby pole is as good as anything else for training cucumbers and peas. Effective trellising enables you to keep plants off the ground and allows you to raise one plant from every few inches of soil. One additional trick to maximize space with cucumbers is to alternate the trellis back and forth for every other plant, so that they grow upward in a V shape. Plants 1, 3, and 5 are encouraged to climb *forward* and upward, while plants 2, 4, and 6 are trained *backward* and upward. Peas and beans can be planted quite closely together, and peas especially are accustomed to being crowded; they will produce well as long as they have enough air circulation to stave off diseases such as mildew.

Tumbling involves growing plants downward from a hanging planter. If you have more airspace than floor space, consider hanging a planter or two from your ceiling, eaves, window ledge, or railing. Strawberries, cherry tomatoes, herbs, and bush beans grow extremely well over the edges of hanging planters, providing you with fresh food that "tumbles" down into your vertical growing space. Although most hanging baskets are designed more for flowers than larger rooting vegetables, you can hang any type of container that can be supported (just remember, wet soil gets quite heavy). Clay pots, buckets, and window boxes all can hang vertically. If you are using a container such as clay that has no holes for hanging, you may want to invest in a hanging basket, or else you can use a few pieces of wire, rope, or twine to create your own supportive cradle for the pot.

A few years ago, a new product appeared on the market called a TopsyTurvy Tomato Planter. The idea was to hang the plant upside down, holding the soil in and then allowing the plant to grow downward and outward toward the light. Although the product was innovative and provided additional support for heavy plants, the basic idea was similar to a hanging grow bag.

To hang a grow bag, you can start with a small bag of soil or purchase an actual grow bag that is made of woven plastic. Several gardening catalogs and Internet sites sell grow bags relatively cheaply, so you can get a dozen or more at once to save on shipping. If you have an extra bag (or partially full bag) of potting soil, tie it up and use some rope or twine to suspend it from a hook or outside rafter where it will get some sun. When the weather is warm enough to plant, wet your soil in the grow bag, cut an "x" in the plastic every few inches, and put in some strawberry seeds or small seedlings. Seedlings may need a little extra support at first, and for this you can use a pipe fitting or some duct tape around the edges. If you hang this over a stairwell or walkway, be sure that it is safely fastened so as not to drop on any passersby. Be sure to keep the bag well watered and use a little liquid fertilizer such as diluted compost tea or kelp extract. It's not the most beautiful container, but with some patience and good fortune you'll soon have some cascading plants that produce delicious, juicy strawberries. What could be more beautiful than that?

Hanging planters of any sort can be a great place for growing cherry tomatoes, strawberries, bush beans, herbs, or even smaller cucumbers. Vinelike veggies that tumble over the side are especially effective at using vertical space. The key is not to plant anything too big, because hanging planters usually are limited in size. Recommended varieties with a trailing habit include "Cool Breeze" cucumbers, "Patio Temptation" strawberries, "Tumbling Tom" or "Tiny Tim" tomatoes, and any variety of bush bean or edible thyme. There are more varieties developed each year for specific purposes such as this, so do not confine yourself to these suggestions. If any fruit gets heavy enough that it threatens to break off, tie it up with some twine or a piece of cloth. In smaller hanging planters, consider growing some edible flowers, herbs, baby salad greens, or wheatgrass for juicing.

USING REFLECTED LIGHT

Reflected light is another powerful concept that has enabled many urban gardens to succeed. Reflected light is indirect sunlight that is bounced off reflective or light-colored surfaces, and it can still bring a lot of energy to your plants. If you want to grow fruiting vegetables such as peppers or tomatoes, but your garden only gets 3 or 4 good hours of sunlight per day, then reflected light might make up the difference.

Gardening beneath a wall can be a great advantage. Walls that are painted white or a light color, particularly stucco walls, reflect a lot of light and heat. They also can shelter a plant from wind and cool night-time temperatures, creating a very favorable microclimate for your plants. In the northern hemisphere, south-facing walls are the most effective for reflecting light and warmth. Walls that face either east or west will pick up some additional early or late light and will translate some of this into warmth. Windows also can reflect light and heat, especially if they face south.

You also can increase your available light by adding your own reflector. This could be a piece of sheet metal, a board painted white, or cardboard covered with aluminum foil. Situate it on the darker side of your plants or in a nearby sunny spot where the light can be reflected back onto your growing space. Be careful with mirrors, glass, or any material that intensely focuses light; these could burn your plants or create a fire danger.

Don't forget artificial light either. Some people grow plants on a balcony or driveway that sits directly under a porch light. If this light source remains on for several hours, perhaps even all night, that extra light energy can generate a lot of additional growth from vegetable plants. Be sure that your light fixture uses compact fluorescent (CFL) lightbulbs. These are much more energy-efficient than regular incandescents, and plants can grow foliage using the type of light they produce.

This raises an additional question: Should you consider using your own artificial lighting? Although hydroponics and indoor greenhouse-style gardening definitely can succeed where the sun does not shine, they are energy-intensive pursuits. Most sustainable gardening advocates would frown on anything more artificial than a lighted grow box for transplants. I would also make an exception for electrical sprouting machines, which use very little energy to produce large amounts of fresh food. But, for all intents and purposes, gardening with artificial light is wasteful unless you have access to renewable energy sources or are using that same light to live by. As the world's energy supplies grow scarcer and more expensive, hydroponics and artificial growing methods are likely to play less of a role.

five

STARTING TRANSPLANTS AND CYCLING YOUR CROPS

Some city residents will read this chapter title and groan. How much more work is involved in starting your own plants from seed? The good news, for those of you who would rather not do this, is that it is optional. You can grow perfectly great crops by sowing seeds directly in the soil where the plant will grow. In some cases, this is the best way to start a new plant. Also, some of you will not plant very many vegetables, and so you may be comfortable going to your local garden center in the springtime and buying vegetable seedlings that someone else has started. This is perfectly acceptable, of course.

However, there are at least three good reasons why you should start your own plants from seed indoors, and then transplant them into their soil for growing. First, it's much cheaper in the long run than buying plants at the nursery. Second, you will have much better choices of what to plant. A given seed catalog may sell three or four varieties of broccoli and dozens of tomatoes, while you will be lucky to find one variety of broccoli and a half-dozen common types of tomatoes at your local nursery. Kohlrabi? Heirloom squash? Mildew-resistant snap peas? Egyptian walking onions? You won't be likely to find these plants sold locally, but the seeds are widely available from mail-order suppliers.

In a small urban garden, perhaps the third reason is the only one that really matters: Starting your own seeds indoors allows you to save time, harvest crops earlier, and rotate plant starts into your garden just when the previous round of veggies is picked. In short, it allows you to produce more from your small growing space. Although a new gardener might want to start off with nursery-raised plant starts, in the long run you should learn to start your own plants from seed. Over time, this is the most affordable, sustainable, and productive option available. If you feel that you will end up spending just as much on extra seeds as you would on nursery seedlings, consider that extra seeds can keep for several years when stored properly in cool, dry, dark conditions.

HOW TO START PLANTS FROM SEED

Starting plants from seed does not have to be difficult or time-consuming. Sure, it will take you a season or two to get the hang of it, but after that the process will seem simple. You will need a space indoors that has natural light from a window, or else a tabletop area above which you can mount a fluorescent light. If you want to start seeds outdoors with climate protection, you could use a grow-frame, plastic cover, or small hobby greenhouse. If you need an indoor light, do not spend the $200 for a hydroponic setup; simply head to your local hardware store and buy a cheap 2- or 4-foot-long fluorescent light that can be mounted under a cabinet or on a chain. The light wavelengths that these bulbs produce will not get you all the way from seed to fruit, but it is sufficient to give your young plants the foliage, roots, and start that they need. Compact fluorescent bulbs (CFLs) are fine as well, though normally these produce a single point of light rather than a row. The row of light works better unless you only plan to start a small handful of seedlings.

Your next step in preparation should be to find out the last average frost date for your location. This is the approximate, but very crucial date that is referred to on the back of many seed packets (for example, "Set plants out three weeks after last average frost date"). To find your last average frost date, check online or with your local nursery or agricultural extension agent. Victory Seed Company has an online frost date selector based on data from the U.S. government; it is available at www.victoryseeds.com/frost. Another online chart is available for major cities from the *Farmer's Almanac* at www.almanac.com/garden/frostus.php (U.S. states) and www.almanac.com/garden/frostcanada.php (Canadian provinces). One warning: Microclimates vary significantly, and in my area a distance of a few miles can extend the frost date by a month. Keep an eye on the temperatures where you live and how much they vary from the closest point listed on those charts. The charts also show the *first* average frost date in the fall, which is good to remember when planning the length of your main growing season.

You will need some containers to start your seeds in. Think of the small seed-starting trays that seedlings come in when you buy them at a nursery; you can either purchase some of these seedling trays, or you can use any other small containers that can be filled with 2 or more inches of seed-starting medium. Small yogurt containers or cutout milk cartons are effective, and you can start a dozen small seedlings in a cardboard egg carton. You also can reuse plastic pots, even larger ones, and plant as many seeds as you can fit in the space. (Do not pack them in too tightly, though, since root growth is important and you will need to get them out without destroying the root system.) Punch a few holes in the bottom of any plastic containers you use to allow for proper drainage, as too much moisture buildup will kill seedlings. Another option is to use peat or coconut (coir) fiber pots, which can be placed right into the garden soil, alleviating some of the stress of transplanting.

For planting times, follow the recommendations on the back of your seed packets coupled with what you have learned about your last frost date. To maximize your chances of success, you can try two or three plantings of the same seeds, each spaced a week or two apart. This way, when your first pepper plants are ready to go in the ground, your next set is only two weeks behind. If it turns out there is a late frost and your first wave of peppers dies, then you have a backup set that's ready to go. Using this method, you can save time and also challenge the seasons with a little more confidence: If you don't stand to lose everything by planting your seedlings early, then you can take some chances on a very early planting.

Put some seed-starting medium into the containers. This can be garden soil, as long as it has enough organic matter to be fairly light, but it should be sifted so that any large pieces of material are kept out. Sifted peat makes a good starter medium and you can also buy good seed-starting potting soil from nurseries (overpriced, but one bag will last you a while). I always mix in a spoonful of compost or worm castings when I start seeds; you do not want to burn young plants with fertilizer, but these amendments are slow to release nutrients and they help strengthen the young plant's immune system. Another option is to use the seed-starting blocks or pellets that are sold by some seed companies and in nurseries.

For anyone using peat products to start seeds indoors, I have two pieces of advice:

1. Some people believe that peat moss is harvested in a manner that is both unsustainable and environmentally irresponsible. If, after examining this issue, you agree, then look for a nursery or online retailer that sells the coconut (coir) fiber alternative, which works just as well and is sustainably harvested. Another company has introduced seed-starting pots made from composted cow manure, which is certainly a renewable resource, and if you cannot find these locally, then check out www.cowpots.com.

2. Peat pots and growing disks often are contaminated with the eggs of root maggots. This can be a big problem if you are growing seedlings in your own home, because you will get little worms eating your seedlings' roots and a cloud of fruit fly-like insects within a few weeks of planting. To sterilize the peat medium before using it, either drench it in a 50/50 solution of water and hydrogen peroxide (give it a day or so to evaporate before planting) or nuke your wet peat products in the microwave for two minutes on high, which also should kill everything. (Keep an eye on it so you don't start a fire since cooking times may vary, and make sure your significant other is not home at the time because your kitchen will smell very earthy.)

Plant the seeds according to the directions on each seed packet. (Do not bother planting beans and peas; they do not transplant well and are better sown directly in the garden.) You can plant two or three seeds per container or block and then thin the plants later, or you can take your chances and just plant one. Early in the season, even indoors, seeds will benefit from some heat and humidity for germination. Putting a plastic bag over the containers is one good way to make this happen. A clear plastic food tray also makes a good cover. Bottom heat speeds up the process and makes it possible to start seeds earlier; you can get a heating pad for seedlings from a nursery or place them on a warm surface such as the top of your refrigerator. As soon as the seedlings start to emerge, take the bag off and start giving them a little light. If you have a sunny window, put them there with a little protection. (A curtain, napkin, or plastic bag well-placed will allow some diffuse sunlight that will not burn young plants.) If you're using a light, your fluorescent or CFL bulb should be on for 12 hours per day (more is okay also), and this should be a few inches from the tops of the seedlings so that they get enough concentrated light. Water the seedlings gently, either from the top of the soil or by placing the seedling containers in a tray of water until their soil seems moist. Make sure they are draining well, and do not overwater; this is a major cause of seedling failure.

Pick only the strongest (bushiest) plants and thin out the spindly and slower-growing ones. Many people suggest that, when the seedlings are up and growing, you run your hands over the leaves whenever you go by to mimic the wind and stimulate the plants to grow stronger in response. A week or so before you plant your seedlings in their final earthly destination, they need to be "hardened off." This is a step that people too often neglect, and it basically means allowing the plant to slowly adjust to the temperature and climate of its new home. You do this by putting the seedlings outside for a short time each day and gradually lengthening this time period. Do not put them in a bright sunny or windy area at first. On the first day, put them outside in filtered sunlight for half an hour. The second day, leave them out for an hour. The third day, leave them out for two hours. Then half a day, then a whole day, bringing them in at night. If they are destined for a windy location, you can begin giving them a little of their customary wind, protected at first if need be. Wind actually can help make a seedling stronger and more vigorous, but only in small doses. After a week of this, let the plant stay out for a whole day and night in its new location, and then plant it the next day. For a peat or coco pot, place it directly in the soil; for other potted seedlings, wet down both the pot's and destination's soil first, then slowly take out the plant with its soil, and be sure not to damage the stem or leaves as you transfer it to its planting hole. If the night temperatures are still near freezing when you set out your plants, then cover each of them at night with a plastic yogurt container, milk carton, or soda bottle that is cut in half: These can make inexpensive season extenders if they help you get your plants in the ground earlier. But when in doubt, do not risk that your plants will freeze: Wait just a little longer to set them out until the frost danger has passed (unless, of course, you have another set of seedlings ready for backup purposes). Before I plant warmer-weather veggies, I always look at the weather report and make sure that their first week in the ground will be a warm one; this helps them get off to a strong start.

If you manage the "hardening off" well and allow the young plant to adapt slowly to its new conditions, then it will produce food for you more quickly than a direct-seeded plant. Using transplants also can allow more growing time for your last cycled crop. But if the plant becomes stressed during transplanting, its yield will drop and it may not survive at all, which negates any time saved from starting it indoors.

CYCLING YOUR CROPS USING TRANSPLANTS

Crop rotation is an important part of organic gardening. We generally are told to rotation-plant vegetables from different families, and not to follow them up with the same plant types again for up to three years. Unfortunately, those of us who garden in containers and small city spaces do not necessarily have this luxury. Luckily, we also do not fall prey to as many soil-borne diseases and pests as do larger-scale gardeners. So it evens out, and in my mind there is no disease or pest that will require me to rotate my city crops.

However, there is another reason to cycle crops, and this is because different types of vegetables have different nutritional requirements. This type of cycling is not done on a year-to-year cycle but a seasonal one, following the nutritional and harvest cycle of the vegetables themselves. Imagine this: Last fall, when you took out the tomatoes, you planted a row of kale seedlings in your largest container, and you and your family feasted on this nutritious (and delicious) leafy green through much of the winter by taking a few leaves from each plant every week. On the coldest nights of the winter, you covered the container with a tarp. Your plants mostly survived the below-freezing temperatures, and even tasted better following a stiff cold snap. Now it is early spring and you've had your fill of kale. You cut off the plants, cook the remaining leaves, and pull up the roots to add to your compost bin. You look at your soil and wonder if you should fertilize again now.

Kale, like many leafy crops, is a heavy nitrogen feeder. Some of the nutrients from your original fertilizer should still be in the soil, but chances are that the nitrogen in this container is very much depleted. Should you add an imbalanced fertilizer with some extra nitrogen to replace what the kale took out?

The answer may be "yes" unless you cycle your crops well. In between the winter greens and the summer fruiting vegetables and the fall roots, you have a small window in the cool spring. It just so happens that peas and beans enrich the soil by adding nitrogen back into it. Fortunately for you, peas like cold weather and bush peas can set a fairly quick crop (in about 55 to 68 days, depending on variety). What if, about a month before the kale is harvested, you planted some bush peas close to the edges of the container? Their roots are shallow and will not compete with the kale. If you use some diluted seaweed extract or seed inoculant (very inexpensive, and available from seed suppliers), these peas and their symbiotic root nodules will fix abundant nitrogen from the air into the soil. When you harvest the kale, the bush peas will already be one month from producing, and then, when it comes time to harvest peas, the seedlings you have started indoors will be ready to place into the nitrogen-replenished soil to become your summer crops. And next time you fertilize again with a balanced organic fertilizer, the nutrient ratios in your soil will still be balanced.

This is an example of cycling some crops for nutritional and seasonal reasons. Also, consider interplanting your crops in the same containers: young chard under tomatoes, interplanted with chives and parsley. A wide range of plants utilizes a wide range of nutrients, and ensures a fairly balanced soil. When deciding which plants to grow at which times of the year, you will be somewhat limited by seasons. For example, tomatoes, peppers, cucumbers, squash, and corn will grow in the summertime, but not at other times, since they need long days and plenty of warmth.

On the other end of the scale, think about what you might be able to grow in the winter; some leafing and even some root crops may do very well in your winter climate. You might even be able to force a crop of potatoes or turnips with some frost protection. In his book *Four-Season Harvest*, Eliot Coleman demonstrates how he grows vegetables year-round in Maine using careful crop selection and a little protection from the elements.[20] He explains how Maine receives as much sunlight in the wintertime as southern France, meaning that much of North America has as much or more light than this famed growing region, even in winter. Making use of row covers, cold frames, or hobby-sized greenhouses, most climates should be capable of raising crops year-round without additional lighting. Although growth slows down significantly with lower temperatures, you can do well with crops such as spinach, arugula, mâche, and scallions, which can grow in the dead of winter with some protection from wind and climate. A small hoop house, cold frame, or even a heavy cover of organic mulch may be enough to protect carrots, parsnips, and leeks. If Coleman can protect and grow his full-scale garden year-round, then you can succeed with a couple of rows or containers. The difference between your own fresh food in the winter versus that lifeless plastic stuff that the supermarket calls lettuce ought to be motivation enough to grow your own greens.

Knowing what you can grow in summer and winter will help you fill out the rest of the seasons. It doesn't take six months to grow a full crop, so do not neglect fall and spring. Radishes, scallions, and salad greens are examples of extremely quick-growing crops that can be harvested within weeks, not months, and along with beans and peas they can fill in some of the transitions when you are between other crops. Using your indoor-raised plant starts, you can reduce the time it takes to grow a crop even more, being ready to introduce a growing plant to the soil each time another crop finishes. Plan out your year in advance, leave a little room for spontaneity, and you will be well on your way to a year-round harvest of fresh food from your own city garden.

six

GROWING FRUIT AND BERRIES IN YOUR SPARE SPACE

Small urban gardeners are not limited to planting vegetables. In recent years, more and more varieties of dwarf and semidwarf fruit trees have been developed, as well as berries for every climate, space, and light level. Many berries and dwarf trees will grow well in containers on a balcony or patio, while a neglected patch of dusty ground next to one's sidewalk may be just enough space to drop in an apple, plum, persimmon, fig, or other fruit tree. Fruit trees make the best of vertical growing because they can utilize a small radius of planting space, and berries of many sorts will fit almost anywhere.

One's ability to grow particular fruits (including berries) largely depends on climate. Basically, fruits can be divided into two main climate categories: temperate fruits and tropical/subtropical fruits. Tropical fruits cannot handle very much winter chill, while temperate fruits require some cool temperatures in the winter (called "chill hours," defined as the total number of hours during which temperatures fall in the 32 to 45 degree F range).[21] The following list shows this breakdown for some common fruits.[22]

TROPICAL/SUBTROPICAL FRUITS	TEMPERATE FRUITS
Avocados	Apples
Bananas	Berries (Blackberries, Blueberries,
Citrus (Lemons, Limes, Oranges, Mandarin	Cranberries, Currants, Raspberries, Strawberries)
Oranges, Kumquats, Grapefruits)	Pears
Guavas	Persimmons
Mangos	Stone Fruits (Apricots, Cherries,
Papayas	Peaches/Nectarines, Plums)
Pineapples	

Luckily, the above list is only a starting point. Although it's true that many tropical fruits will grow only in warm locations and many temperate fruits need a certain number of winter chill hours to set fruit, there are many fruits that can grow well in a wide range of climates. The following list shows some fruits, with notes on particular varieties, that can grow well in moderate climate ranges.

SOME FRUITS THAT CAN GROW WELL IN A RANGE OF CLIMATES

APPLES: There are many hundreds of varieties, some of which will grow almost anywhere. Northern gardeners are blessed with a wide range of selections, including winter-hardy types such as Honeycrisp, McIntosh, Golden Delicious, Haralson, and Northern Spy. Warm-climate gardeners can try low-chill varieties such as Anna, Beverly Hills, Cox's Orange Pippin, Dorset Golden, Fuji, Gala, Pettingill, and Esopus Spitzenburg, all of which have proven successful in southern California.[23] Anna, Dorset, and Tropic Sweet can even be grown in parts of Florida.[24]

BLACKBERRIES AND RASPBERRIES: Berry canes can be trained up walls or trellises; they are vigorous growers and heavy berry producers. Many kinds of blackberries grow wild throughout North America, and others have been optimized for flavor, particular climates, or thornless characteristics. Check with local and mail-order nurseries for more information. Raspberries grow naturally in a more limited geographic range, needing some chill hours and being less tolerant of hot, humid climates. Southern gardeners should check with a local nursery about the varieties with the best chances of success in their gardening zones.[25]

BLUEBERRIES: Originally adapted for northern climates, there are several low-chill varieties that will grow well elsewhere. If it rarely snows in your region, check nurseries and mail-order catalogs for the low-chill Southern Highbush varieties such as Misty, O'Neal, Reveille, and Sharpblue. Northern gardeners have many more choices, which are widely available at nurseries. Blueberries also make great container plants.

DRAGONFRUIT (PITAYA/PITAHAYA): Here is a newly popular subtropical cactus that can be raised in containers for its nutritious and extremely exotic-looking fruit. The fruits are either red-purple, pink, or light green, and have a pleasant taste with seeds that give it an appearance like a kiwi. The plant does not like particularly hot summer temperatures and it tolerates short frosts, though the cactus plant can sustain damage at temperatures much below freezing.[26] Growers in a moderate temperature range might want to give it a try, and anyone with a sunny window could move the container indoors during the winter to avoid frost damage. Researchers have begun to study this plant only recently and there appear to be at least 60 different varieties, some of which may handle cooler temperatures. Look for the seeds or cuttings at nurseries that sell cacti or succulents. For mail orders, Flora Exotica in Quebec (www.floraexotica.ca) sells live plants and Trade Winds Fruit in California (www.tradewindsfruit.com) provides seeds. Rivers End Nursery in Texas (www.riversendnursery.com) will sell either cuttings or seeds.

FIGS: Here is a subtropical fruit that is not particular about latitude. Some varieties can handle the cold, going dormant and returning with vigor the following year, such as the Hardy Chicago fig, which has been grown from New York to Sweden. To protect trees from winter damage, prune them to bush form, and wrap with a burlap bag. Better yet, you can grow figs in containers and move them indoors during harsh winters.[27]

GRAPES: There are numerous varieties of wine and table grapes. Check local nurseries for suitable types for your area. Like cane berries, grapes can be grown vertically up a wall or trellis, perhaps at the edge of one's sidewalk or patio. Container growing is another possibility.

JUJUBES: Yes, candy does grow on trees. Sometimes known as Chinese date, the jujube is sweet and can be eaten fresh or dried. Like figs, the trees are subtropical yet can stand some subfreezing temperatures. The California Rare Fruit Growers organization reports that various jujube cultivars have fruited from Pennsylvania to the Pacific Northwest and as far south as Florida.[28] Try One Green World in Oregon (www.onegreenworld.com), Bay Laurel Nursery in California (www.baylaurelnursery.com), Hidden Springs Nursery in Tennessee (www.hiddenspringsnursery.com), or Johnson Nursery in Georgia (www.johnsonnursery.com) for some selections. Smaller varieties can be container grown.

KIWIS (INCLUDING HARDY KIWIS): Nearly anyone can grow either regular (fuzzy) kiwis or their smaller and freeze-tolerant counterparts, Hardy Kiwis. Fuzzy kiwis grow well in areas where citrus can be grown. For northern gardeners, the berry-sized Hardy Kiwis can extend the range of this perennial and are sold by nurseries in states as cold as Iowa and Illinois.[29] [30] The One Green World nursery, referenced above, has collected Hardy Kiwi and Arctic Beauty Kiwi vines from Siberia, which are hardy to -35 degrees F. (Yes, that's a minus sign.) Kiwis grow as vines and take some space; they can be trained up a strong trellis or arbor. Both a female and male plant are needed for pollination.

MELONS: Don't forget that melons, which grow like squash, are terrific fruit. If you have enough space and a dose of summer heat, this may be a good crop for you. There are dozens of varieties, and some may be grown effectively on a vertical trellis.

PEARS (INCLUDING ASIAN PEARS): These will grow in many parts of the country and in many soil types, though they are prone to disease. Like apples, most pear varieties require some chill hours. Low-chill varieties include Monterrey, Hood, and Kieffer, and some have reported success with Bartlett and Seckel in cool maritime climates.[31] The Asian pears (rounder and crunchy like an apple) are generally low-chill, but require warm summers to fully ripen.

PERSIMMONS: The American varieties are native to much of the eastern two-thirds of the country, from Connecticut to Florida, Texas to Iowa.[32] The Asian varieties, especially Hachiya (soft when ripe) and Fuyu (ripe when firm; eaten like an apple) are becoming more familiar to many supermarket shoppers. The Hachiya and Fuyu are each self-fruitful, meaning that you only need one tree for pollination, and both are widely available from nurseries and mail-order catalogs or Web sites.[33]

PINEAPPLE GUAVA (FEIJOA): Although it won't take to the snow, the Pineapple Guava thrives in cooler temperatures than the more tropical guava (to which it is distantly related). It is a slow-growing shrub with tasty, kiwi-sized fruit and is worth trying in northern California and the maritime Northwest, northern Florida, and parts of the Southeast. With protection from cold winters and/or hot summer sun, it may also thrive in other microclimates.[34] These trees are becoming much more common at neighborhood nurseries, and you may be able to special order Feijoa if they do not stock it regularly.

LOQUATS: Hardy to 20 degrees F, loquats will grow in warmer parts of the country or with frost protection, and will set fruit when grown in large containers.[35] The fruit is orange and apricot-sized with white to orange flesh that ranges from tart to sweet.[36] One advantage to growing a loquat tree is that it fruits in the late winter or spring in the Northern Hemisphere (depending on the cultivar and location), providing an early-season source of fruit.[37] See the advice on growing figs in containers, which also applies here.

PAWPAWS: This is a native North American fruit that can provide a touch of the exotic to even colder climates. It is hardy down to around -25 degrees F. Some describe the fruit as tasting something like a banana, pineapple, or vanilla custard, but this varies according to the variety and the taster. Pawpaw trees are naturally small trees and can grow in partial shade as an understory tree. Kentucky State University has compiled a list of different varieties, which is available at www.pawpaw.kysu.edu/pawpaw/cvsrc98.htm, and a good local nursery or extension agent also may be able to recommend the best ones for you to try based on climate. Pollination of pawpaws can be problematic both in nature and in urban gardens, so to help ensure decent production, you should plant at least two different cultivars or seedlings. In some urban gardens, due to fewer winged insects, you may have to hand-pollinate the flowers using a paintbrush.

PLUMS: This is the most adaptable stone fruit. Though there are wild varieties, most plums that we know today are either European or Asian varieties. European plums, which include prunes, Damsons, Stanley, and Green Gage types, grow well in areas with strong winter chill.[38] If you live far enough south, where late spring frosts are rare, or do not have many chill hours, an Asian/Japanese plum or Pluot may be better. Check nurseries for varieties such as Santa Rosa, Methley, Shiro, Satsuma, and Burgundy. The plum-apricot hybrids known as Pluots are incredibly sweet and tend to favor their plum heritage in terms of flavor.

OTHER STONE FRUIT: These generally grow in more limited climate ranges. Peaches and nectarines cannot grow in the far north or the subtropical south because they are not very cold hardy, yet they also require summer heat to ripen. Check with your local nursery for varieties that may grow well in your area. There are a few low-chill varieties of apricots available from nurseries, such as Gold Kist and Katy. For northern gardeners with late spring frosts, look for late-blooming apricots such as Puget Gold and Sub Zero. Cherries are more successful in their native climate range, requiring cold winters to set fruit. Possible substitutes for warmer climates include native chokecherries, wild plums, bush cherries, Nanking cherries, and Capulin cherries, none of which is quite as tasty.

STRAWBERRIES: You can grow these in containers or ground-based beds. There are many varieties available today that will thrive in different climates. Check with a nursery or mail-order supplier to see what varieties they recommend for your region. For shady spots, consider growing Alpine Strawberries (see p. 71).

CONTAINER GROWING FOR SMALL FRUITS AND BERRIES

Even if you have no ground to plant, you can grow small fruit trees and berries in containers. Some fruits and berries that naturally grow well in containers include figs, blueberries, and strawberries, but the fun does not end there. Dwarf fruit trees provide urban gardeners with a lot of options these days, including natural genetic dwarf varieties of cherries and nectarines, as well as apples and pears that are grafted onto dwarfing rootstock. In climates that will support citrus growing, a dwarf lemon, lime, or mandarin orange will provide plenty of vitamin C for your family in late fall and well into winter. Avocados and pineapple guava (feijoa) also can be grown in containers where climates support citrus.

Growing in containers also allows you to move your trees or bushes according to where they get the most light. I used to garden on a balcony, for example, that had summer light on the left side and winter light on the right side, so I would move some of my planters according to the season. To make this task easier and prevent a back injury, you could get a planter base with wheels. I have not used these, but have seen them sold at nurseries for only a few dollars. Placing your potted tree atop one of these bases will allow you to have an ambulatory container without needing an ambulance for yourself.

PROPER POLLINATION IN THE MINI-ORCHARD

One major issue with small-scale and container-grown fruit is proper pollination. There are two potential problems here. First, there is a risk that honeybees or other friendly flying insects will not find your mini-orchard, which may be surrounded by an urban jungle of concrete, glass, and steel. Short of starting your own hive of bees, the best bet here

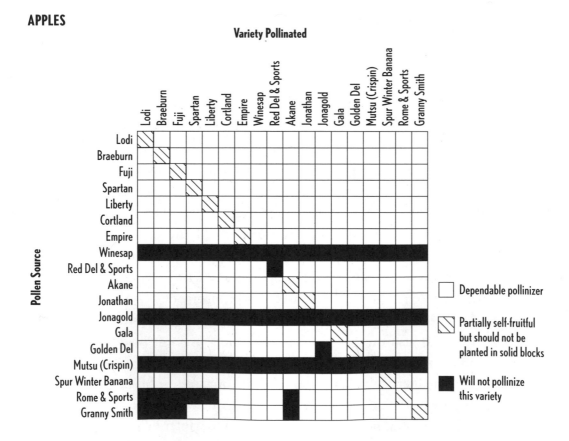

APPLES

Recreated with permission from Colorado State University Extension, fact sheet no. 7.002, Pollination of Fruit Trees, by A. Gaus; for more information visit www.ext.colostate.edu

is to plant something else that bees or other friendlies find irresistible and that flowers around the same time as your fruit trees. A few herbs or the right flowers may do the trick. You should ask a local nursery or extension agent to find out what to plant for this purpose, or you can experiment.

Pollination problem #2 is that, although some fruit trees are self-fertile, others need a second tree of a different variety for pollination. This is the case with many varieties of apples, for example. The popular Golden Delicious and Granny Smith varieties are examples of two cultivars that are considered self-fruitful (in other words, just one tree will set fruit on its own). However, having a second tree of another variety improves production. On the other end of the spectrum, there are apples such as Gravenstein and Belle de Boskoop that are pollen-sterile, meaning they need another variety as a pollinator, and cannot serve as pollinators for other trees. Most types of apples fall somewhere in between, needing a second tree for pollination, but being able to serve as pollinator for that second tree, assuming they bloom at the same time. Confused? If you have room for just one tree, make sure you get one that is labeled as "self-fertile" or "self-fruitful." Most of these also can pollinate a second tree that blooms around the same time. If you plan to get more than two trees, or are not sure of the varieties' bloom times,

PEARS

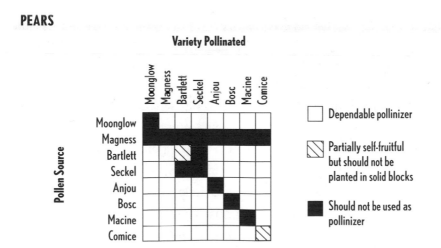

Recreated with permission from Colorado State University Extension, fact sheet no. 7.002, Pollination of Fruit Trees, by A. Gaus; for more information visit www.ext.colostate.edu

SWEET CHERRIES

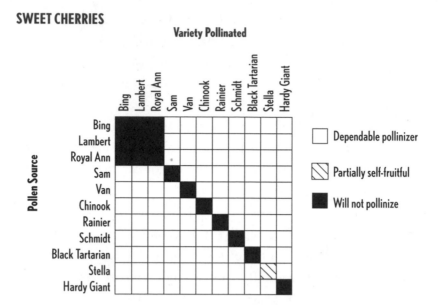

Recreated with permission from Colorado State University Extension, fact sheet no. 7.002, Pollination of Fruit Trees, by A. Gaus; for more information visit www.ext.colostate.edu

then consider planting a crabapple, many of which flower continuously throughout the blooming season and are good for pollinating any other apple. Although most crabapples are sour and barely edible, there are some wonderfully sweet ones available, such as Chestnut, Whitney, and Centennial. Other kinds, such as Dolgo, may still be useful for jelly and sauce, if not for fresh eating.

Most other types of fruit trees are similar in that they either need, or produce better with, a second variety of tree nearby. So the advice for apples remains the same as for other fruit: If you are able to fit only a single tree, get one that is supposed to be "self-fertile" or "self-fruitful." If one of your close neighbors has another variety of tree, located no more than 100 feet away, then this may be enough to get the job done. When planning to plant two fruit trees for pollination, it pays to research your chosen fruit and its varieties, some of which serve as reliable pollinators while others do not. The preceding and following charts show some major fruits and their pollination capabilities: apples, pears, sweet cherries, and plums.

PLUMS

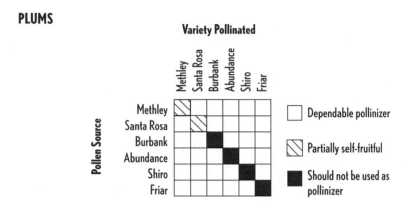

Recreated with permission from Colorado State University Extension, fact sheet no. 7.002, Pollination of Fruit Trees, by A. Gaus; for more information visit www.ext.colostate.edu

PLANTING MULTIPLE TREES IN A SMALL SPOT

Once upon a time, when someone grew a tree, the conventional wisdom was to give it a huge growing area and let it grow as big as possible. This was how commercial orchards were planted, and the old fruit tree behind someone's house would eventually grow large enough that you would need to climb it in order to harvest it. I have wonderful memories of climbing such trees as a kid and harvesting impossible quantities of fresh cherries, apples, and persimmons.

Luckily for the small urban gardener, times have changed. Growers today understand, and even recommend, that you plant several fruit trees close together and keep them pruned small for maximum production. Many commercial apple orchards, which once grew giant trees far apart from one another, have replaced their older trees with more closely spaced semidwarf and dwarf trees. The idea behind this is to economize, make harvesting easier, and ultimately get more dependable fruit production from a given space. It also turns out that planting similar varieties just a few feet (even inches!) apart helps to dwarf the tree and mildly stress it so that it fruits earlier and more heavily.

This arrangement is more economical for city growers who have limited space, and it allows us to squeeze in some different varieties of fruit. For example, in a 10 x 10-foot ground space, you could squeeze in four trees, which you would space 18 inches apart. If you planted pears, rather than having a single pear tree that produced hundreds of pounds of one type of pear ripening all at once, you could have four different varieties that would ripen at different times all summer. This rolling harvest would give you more manageable quantities of pears ripening in mid-July, late July, August, and September. And if this still sounds like too many pears, then pears and apples can be planted together, and stone fruits (peaches, nectarines, plums, and cherries) can share the same space. One longtime nurseryman, who was initially skeptical about intensive orchard planting, finally concluded, "What convinced me was that you could have fresh fruit for five months out of the year, perhaps June through October."[39] This in manageable amounts, from a small space, and from trees that are pruned no higher than arm's reach for ease of harvest. For home growers interested in some photos and diagrams of proven tree spacing ideas, I encourage you to visit the Web site of Dave Wilson Nursery (www.davewilson.com), a premier wholesale fruit tree nursery that preaches intensive planting and includes a plethora of free information about it.

CONTAINER GROWING TIPS

Here are some thoughts about growing particular fruits and berries from containers. This is not a complete list, but it covers many common fruits and berries that can be grown in containers. Other types of fruits may be dwarfed or pruned to container-growing size as well, so if you don't see your favorite fruit here, don't despair. Do some research, find out what others have done, and experiment for yourself. You may learn something valuable to share with other aspiring urban gardeners and orchardists!

Apples and pears: A mature dwarf tree can bear as much as 50 to 100 pounds of fruit per year.[40] Apple cultivars of your choice can be grafted onto dwarfing rootstock such as M9, M27, or Bud-9, which keep the trees somewhere around 25 percent of their normal height at maturity.[41] Humans have been grafting apples for thousands of years as a means of propagating these trees.[42] For pears, which are closely related, look for any varieties that are grafted to dwarfing quince or

OHxF rootstocks to keep the trees small.[43] Numerous nurseries sell dwarfing apples and pears; if your nursery person does not know what a rootstock is, turn around and walk out the door. Some good mail-order sources include Bay Laurel Nursery in California (www.baylaurelnursery.com), Vintage Virginia Apples (www.virginiavintageapples.com) in Virginia, Cummins Nursery in New York (www.cumminsnursery.com), Raintree Nursery in Washington (www.raintreenursery.com), and Stark Brothers in Missouri (www.starkbros.com). Finally, even dwarf apples and pears can grow 10 to 12 feet tall and nearly as wide, so if you have a truly small space and a container, consider one of the newer columnar apples. These are small, vertical trees, which can fit in a pot or very small ground space. Look for columnar varieties such as Scarlett Sentinel Columnar, Northpole Columnar, and Golden Sentinel Columnar. You may need two varieties for pollination.

Blueberries: Many types of blueberries grow well in containers. A 20-inch pot is big enough for one full plant, but you'll need to grow at least two different varieties for optimum fruit production. They like acid soil, so be sure to use plenty of peat and a little soil sulfur to lower the pH. Ed Laivo of Dave Wilson Nursery, one of the nation's premier wholesale fruit tree growers, recommends a mix of 1/3 pathway bark, 1/3 peat moss, and 1/3 humus-based potting soil along with two tablespoons of soil sulfur, then a high-nitrogen fertilizer in the springtime.[44]

Other berries: Strawberries grow well in containers of all sizes. You can grow them along with vegetables. If you intend to really pack in the plants, then deeper containers will give them enough soil space for their roots; shallow window boxes and so-called strawberry pots can really crowd the roots and hamper production (see Chapter 3, p. 27). Blackberries and raspberries grow on canes, and therefore need some vertical support from a trellis. These can be good fruit producers when grown from containers or in a neglected patch of ground. They require very little attention other than regular watering and pruning. One warning: When planted in the ground, cane berries can sucker and spread quickly, so keep an eye on them, and keep them where you want them. There are many other wonderful berries that can grow in containers, including currants, gooseberries, lingonberries, huckleberries, wintergreen, and cranberries. For an extensive selection of mail-order berry plants and fruiting shrubs that will open your mind to new possibilities, try Raintree Nursery in Washington (www.raintreenursery.com), One Green World in Oregon (www.onegreenworld.com), Nourse Farms in Massachusetts (www.noursefarms.com), Stark Brothers in Missouri (www.stark bros.com), Sandusky Valley Nursery in Ohio (www.svnursery.com), or Hartmann's Plant Company in Michigan (www.hartmannsplant company.com).

Citrus: If you live in citrus country, your local nurseries should carry dwarf varieties of lemons, limes, oranges, mandarin oranges, grapefruit, kumquats, and more. Lemons, limes, and mandarins can handle slightly cooler summers than oranges and grapefruits. North of the citrus belt, you may want to experiment with indoor dwarf citrus that are grown near a sunny window; try Dwarf Improved Meyer Lemon or Dwarf Satsuma Mandarin Orange.

Figs: Growing figs in containers provides all the advantages of having a larger fig tree, though the fruit yields will be substantially less. The larger the container, the more the tree can grow. A half whiskey barrel or wine barrel size is optimum, but even a 5-gallon bucket with good soil and drainage holes can grow a small tree and yield a few handfuls of fresh fruit. If you have space for several such containers on a balcony or patio, then you can get as many figs as someone with a larger tree. As the fig tree grows, make sure that the container does not tip over in the wind. Figs like heat, so placement on a south-facing wall, if you have one, is ideal. In early winter, prune the tree back enough so that you can wrap it with some protective burlap or cover it with straw, compost, or newspaper. (Don't worry, it will grow back with a vengeance next season.) In cold winter areas, container trees may be moved indoors to protect them from the elements.

Stone fruit: There are a few natural (genetic) dwarf varieties available, as well as more widely known cultivars that have been grafted onto dwarfing rootstock and sold as dwarf trees. Try them in containers or on small patches of ground. Burgess Seed and Plant Company sells a variety of these, including Dwarf North Star Cherry, Dwarf Red Haven Peach, Dwarf Nectarine, and Dwarf Damson and Stanley Plums (www.eburgess.com). Stark Brothers sells a July Elberta Peach Dwarf,

Dwarf Methley and Shiro Plums, and at least a dozen more varieties of dwarfing stone fruit cultivars (www.starkbros.com). Gurney's features a Carmine Jewel Dwarf Cherry and others (www.gurneys.com).

Warmer-climate choices: These include dwarf pomegranates and bananas. Guavas and papayas also make good container fruit plants. In tropical areas, there is a seemingly endless variety of exotics, many of which can be grown as small trees in containers. Check with your local nursery or the North American Fruit Explorers (www.nafex.org) for more information.

USING NEGLECTED GROUND SPACE

Before using all your available patio or balcony space for fruit trees (rather than vegetables or other uses), take stock of whether you have *any* available patch of ground in which to plant a tree or berry bush. A dusty patch of soil next to a sidewalk or in the corner of a patio may be a possible home for an apple, fig, plum, or blueberry. If you own the property or can get permission to do so, you may be able to remove a couple of pathway stones, a mailbox, or a flower planter to make room for fruit or berries. Many fruit trees and berry bushes do not need much horizontal space or care; some are drought-tolerant and do not require regular watering after they are established. Where horizontal space is at a premium, trees make the best use of vertical areas with their below-ground roots and aboveground fruiting branches.

LOW LIGHT BERRIES

A central problem for many of us who garden in the city is a lack of light. This is covered extensively in the vegetable chapters. I mention it again here only to note the problem that shade poses for growing fruit. In short, most fruit trees require nearly a full day of sunlight in order to set and ripen fruit. So what can you do if your only available growing space gets only a few hours of light per day? Here I have two pieces of advice: First, if you are gardening in the southern United

© istockphoto.com/ftwitty

States or anywhere with hot weather, then this small bit of sun might be enough, since some trees prefer partial shade in hot summers and can even get burned in full sun. So be courageous and try planting something there. Second, there are a few berries that are proven to be good shade producers, so you can try one of these even in partial shade conditions. In their natural environment, as lower-growing shrubs in woodland areas, many berry plants are used to partial shade. Blackberries, for example, can set nearly a full crop on a few hours of sunlight per day, and other, less common types of berries are solid shade producers as well.

Huckleberries, a wild predecessor of domesticated blueberries, grow throughout much of North America. You have probably come across wild berries while hiking at some point in your life, yet although you and I may not feel safe trying them in the wild, huckleberries and other wild berries have long been staples for Native American tribes, as well as forage for bears, birds, and other wildlife.[45] On the West Coast, we have a several native varieties of huckleberry, including a variety called evergreen huckleberry, which grows well in the shade.[46] It is one of the rare berries that actually grows better in the shade than in the sun, still produces delicious fruit, and is not particular about soil type. In other parts of the country, you may want to investigate whether you have native huckleberries that can grow in shady conditions.

Gardeners in the Midwest, Rocky Mountains, Northeast, and Northwest have other berry options as well. These include currants and the closely related gooseberries. Currants are the better known of the two, with several native varieties growing wild and a long history of cultivation in Europe and the Eastern states. Gooseberries, which are easy to grow and just as delicious, can be planted under fruit trees and still bear successfully in less than full sunlight.[47] According to the University of Minnesota Extension, both currant and gooseberry plants can perform very well in as little as a half day of sunlight.[48] Both grow on canes, much like blackberries and raspberries, but are not often trellised (though they can be). The canes can be pruned as necessary for smaller space gardens. You can order these plants, either bareroot or potted, from many local and mail-order nurseries. Because black currants were once known as a host for the disease white pine blister rust, some Northeastern and Midwestern states outlawed them. Most of these states now permit disease-resistant varieties; check with your nursery or a reputable mail-order supplier for some suggestions.

Other low-growing berries are also worth trying, since their natural habitats are partially shady. Anything that grows as a groundcover (alpine strawberry, cranberry, bearberry) or low-growing shrub (lingonberry, lowbush blueberry, creeping Taiwan raspberry) may bear successfully in limited sunlight. If you have a patch of yard that is mainly shady and space enough for a larger shrub, consider an elderberry. These beautiful bushes thrive in partial shade to produce healthful fruit that makes delicious wine and preserves. Hidden Springs Nursery (www.hiddenspringsnursery.com), Raintree Nursery (www.raintreenursery.com), and One Green World (www.onegreenworld.com) have an especially wide selection of unusual and edible berries.

USING TRELLISES, WALLS, AND ESPALIERS TO GROW FRUIT

Your space is limited, so you must use it well. It is normally not too difficult to keep small trees and berry bushes pruned. This involves pruning off any dead or excess growth during the winter with the aim of helping the tree maximize its energy into growing its main branches and producing good fruit. Pruning also can help promote good air circulation and sunlight for the branches. If you have a particular space that the tree must fit, you can prune most types of small trees to fit your space.

Growing fruit or berries on trellises can help you train these plants vertically and maximize your space. Simple, two-dimensional trellises often are sold in nurseries and commonly take the shape of a fan or lattice. If you have a south-facing wall, consider training a fruit tree to grow two-dimensionally to maximize your space. Apples, pears, grapes, and figs are examples of plants that can be espaliered (trained and pruned to grow two-dimensionally, often into specific shapes and forms). This is fairly simple to do, and a free Internet search for "espalier" will show you some different patterns to try. Your local library may

A large 3-D trellis for container-grown kiwi plants. ©iStockphoto.com/drw0649

A pear tree espaliered along a wall with a lattice. ©iStockphoto.com/iFotoman

have a book on backyard gardening or small orchard management that includes a chapter on espalier. One good book that I found at a local library is *The Complete Guide to Pruning and Training Plants* by David Joyce and Christopher Brickell of England's Royal Horticultural Society.[49]

Other fruit grows better on a larger trellis. For vining fruits (such as grapes and kiwi) and cane berries (such as raspberries, blackberries, currants, and gooseberries), you will get more fruit with a three-dimensional trellis. Imagine a vineyard, where a row of grapes grows between posts. Their vines are trained along wires or horizontal supports that are strung between the posts. These must be strong enough, and widely spaced, to support heavy vines laden with fruit. Next, imagine an arbor.

Vertical grapes growing on a shaded street in Europe, making the best of small patches of soil and growing up each wall toward the light. ©iStockphoto.com/lianeremmler

It is basically four posts with a stepladder placed horizontally on top of them, and perhaps some lattices on each end. Arbors make great trellises because they support three-dimensional growth: upward, across, and outward. What you need for vine or cane fruits, even in a container garden, is a smaller version of these. You can make a simple 3-D trellis above planter boxes by taking four posts and stringing some strong fencing wire around the top corners to make a rectangular frame on top. You can nail the posts to wooden containers or sink them into the ground or container-based soil. Grapes and kiwis will be trained to grow up and then along the wires, while cane berries will be planted into the soil underneath and will grow up through (inside) the rectangular wire frame. This is like gathering flowers in a bouquet rather than setting them flat on a table: Keeping the canes inside the wire frame will prevent spreading and help the berries grow vertically in your small space, allowing maximum berry production and easy harvesting. 3-D trellises can be used above a single large container or several small ones.

PRESERVING THE BOUNTY

When it rains, it pours. If you have an excess of fruit or berries, whether from your garden or other sources, you may want to preserve some of it for leaner times. Fruit can be frozen, dried, pickled, canned, fermented, or made into juice, jam, or pie. Although it is easy enough for a novice grower to freeze extra fruit or follow a pie recipe, you may need some training on other methods of preservation. There are a number of good books that can teach you how to do this successfully; I will recommend two here. *Putting Food By* by Janet Greene, Ruth Hertzberg, and Beatrice Vaughan is a classic guide to canning, drying, pickling, and other methods of preservation. It is particularly helpful for its step-by-step guide to proper and hygienic canning procedures for different foods.[50] However, canning requires boiling and a large output of energy, so anyone interested in less intensive methods of preserving will rejoice at a wonderful new book called *Preserving Food Without Freezing or Canning* by the Gardeners and Farmers of Centre Terre Vivante in France.[51] This book reintroduces age-old methods of traditional food preservation that

Dwarf apple tree bearing fruit from a container. ©iStockphoto.com/AtWaG

do not require high energy. I highly recommend it to anyone wanting to learn these traditional techniques; they will allow you to make the bounty of a summer harvest last for much of the year.

FORAGING AND TRADING

Not far from my home there is a park with trails that are lined with blackberry bushes. In the fall, these are covered with more berries than the birds can eat. It is a simple matter to fill up some baskets and containers with enough blackberries for my family, and after eating our fill, we still have enough left over to make some blackberry jam. Even in the city, fruit trees often grow on abandoned lots or on property where the owner does not care for them. Keep an eye out for that old apple tree or scrubby chokecherry bush that can provide you with armloads of fresh fruit. You may need permission to harvest from someone else's land, but if you offer them a couple of jars of applesauce or a cherry pie, they won't be likely to refuse. Jeff Ball, author of *The Self-Sufficient Suburban Garden*, also suggests that you can learn the simple trade of caring for fruit trees (consisting mainly of regular pruning), and offer to care for any neighbors' neglected trees in your area in exchange for half the fruit.[52]

My point is this: In planning my garden, I know that I will never need to grow blackberries. You too may have access to fresh fruit without having to grow it. So take stock of what is available in your vicinity and factor this into your garden planning. Then you can focus on raising food crops that complement, rather than duplicate, what is already available in your neighborhood. Also consider what your neighbors are growing and may have in excess; for example, if someone you know has a persimmon tree or is always trying to give away extra summer squash, you might focus on some other crops that mature at a different time and trade with neighbors to complement your diet.

Most urban areas are in close proximity to parks or surrounding natural areas that may offer you access to wild fruits and vegetables. Especially in lean times, foraging can constitute an important part of your seasonal food supply. If you want to educate yourself more on food from wild sources, I urge you to invest in a guide to your region's edible plants. A good beginning book for all aspiring foragers, particularly those in the Great Lakes, Northeast, and Eastern Canadian regions, is *The Forager's Harvest* by Samuel Thayer.[53] This book not only explains some common varieties of edible plants but also helps the reader build confidence in selecting, gathering, and preparing food from wild plants. After reading this book, try to find a field guide to your area's edible plants, and make sure that it has detailed photographs or drawings to help you identify the truly edible plants as well as similar-looking ones you should avoid.

seven

SPROUTING GRAINS, BEANS, WHEATGRASS, AND SALAD SPROUTS

"Wanted! A vegetable that will grow in any climate, will rival meat in nutritive value, will mature in 3 to 5 days, may be planted any day of the year, will require neither soil nor sunshine, will rival tomatoes in vitamin C, will be free of waste in preparation, and can be cooked with little fuel and as quickly as a . . . chop." Dr. Clive McKay, a Nutrition Professor at Cornell University, used this announcement to begin his study of sprouts, which contain more nutrients per calorie than any other type of food.

While living in the city, I too have become a big advocate of sprouting. Quite simply, it allows me to produce armloads of fresh food every week, from pennies' worth of seed, using just one or two square feet of space that does not need to be well lighted. No other food production system can claim this. Sprouts can be eaten raw or cooked, used in salads, sandwiches, or stir-fries, and some can be juiced as well. The most common seeds to sprout are alfalfa, broccoli, radish, clover, mung bean, soybean, lentil, wheatgrass, and other grains. Nutrition from sprouts is second to none, with more and more studies attesting to this each year.

Sprouts retain the nutrition from their seeds and create much more. Radish sprouts contain 29 times more vitamin C than milk, 10 times more calcium than a potato, and more vitamin C than a pineapple.[54] Mung bean and soybean sprouts, which are staples of East Asian cooking, contain nearly 50 percent more protein than their dry seeds. They retain the B vitamin content from their seeds, while the sprouts in their first few days more than double the amount of vitamins A and C in the dry bean.[55] One cup of soybean sprouts contains only 86 calories, yet satisfies 9 percent of your body's daily requirement for protein, plus 3 percent of your dietary fiber, 18 percent of your vitamin C, 8 percent of your iron, and 30 percent of your folate needs.[56] Through the process of sprouting, the starches and proteins in grains and beans are broken down into simple sugars and amino acids, which are simpler for the body to digest, and their high enzymatic value makes them arguably the healthiest fresh food on the planet.[57] People with weakened immune systems may want to avoid certain types of fresh sprouts, such as alfalfa sprouts, which also can contain high levels of phytotoxins (natural, plant-produced substances that can suppress immune system function).

Most people are familiar with alfalfa sprouts, which are commonly used on sandwiches. Few people, however, know that they pack an incredible nutritional punch. According to the U.S. Department of Agriculture, two 100-gram servings of alfalfa sprouts contain more than 6 percent of your recommended daily allowance (RDA) of vitamin A, 14 percent of your vitamin C, healthy doses of riboflavin, niacin, and other B vitamins, and nearly half a day's dose of vitamin K. In addition, these sprouts are very high in iron and zinc and contain significant amounts of other essential minerals such as calcium, magnesium, and potassium.[58] Recent studies have shown that alfalfa, clover, broccoli, flaxseed, and soybean sprouts are nature's richest sources of isoflavones, coumestans, and lignins, which play an important role in the prevention of breast and colon cancer, heart disease, osteoporosis, and menopausal symptoms.[59] Broccoli contains a substance that may be thousands of times more powerful than antioxidants in fighting heart disease. However, according to a University of Saskatchewan study, it would be nearly impossible for most people to eat enough broccoli per day to give them a substantial benefit. Broccoli sprouts, on the other hand, contain 20 to 50 times more of this substance than the mature plant, meaning that a handful or two per day may allow your body to "correct major cardiovascular dysfunctions such as hypertension and stroke" according to the study's lead author.[60]

There are at least three major questions for anyone thinking about sprouting. First, how difficult is it and how much time does it take? Second, what can I grow? And third, how will I eat all those sprouts? The remainder of this chapter seeks to answer these questions and to help you get started with sprouting.

How difficult is sprouting and how much time does it take? Sprouts can grow with no soil or light, and they will be ready within 4 to 10 days, depending on what kind of seeds you sprout. So, basically, the process itself is very quick and you can produce fresh vegetables in just days instead of months. In terms of your time commitment, it will require a few minutes each day to rinse the sprouts to prevent mold. If you decide to invest in an automatic sprouting system, then this will keep your sprouts well rinsed; you will just need to change the water every day or so to keep it fresh. Home sprouting in your own controlled environment allows you to avoid contamination risks associated with commercially-grown sprouts. In terms of equipment, you can either start with what you have at home or purchase a more specialized sprouting device. To use readily available materials and save money, you can start with either a glass jar or a plastic seedling tray. A cloth bag that is wet, warm, and filled with bean seeds also can work if you rinse it regularly. Regardless of what kind of equipment you use, all of it should be well washed beforehand and you should plan to rinse your sprouts about three times per day as they grow. (It will take less than one minute each time.)

A glass jar is by far the easiest way to experiment with sprouting seeds. To sprout in a glass jar, you will need to cover it with something that can hold in the seeds when you rinse them. A screen held on with a rubber band should work well. First, put a handful of the seeds you want to sprout (alfalfa, mung beans, etc.) in the bottom of the jar. Fill the jar partway with cool water, and allow the seeds to soak for about 8 hours. Then pour out the water through the screen and refill it with enough water to rinse the seeds. Repeat the rinsing part again, and try to drain out as much of the water as possible. Leave the seeds to sprout and return to rinse them this way about three times each day. In only a few days, you should have some yummy sprouts!

Growing on a seedling tray requires that you use some type of growing medium that mimics soil. Actually, there is no rule against using soil itself, which can provide both support and a little nutrition to the sprouts. Stick to sterilized soil, or put some in the microwave and cook on high power for two minutes to kill any pathogens. Other soilless mediums for sprouting can include perlite or asbestos-free vermiculite, which may be available at your local garden center. Theoretically, you

Alfalfa, adzuki bean, broccoli, and sunflower sprouts. ©iStockphoto.com/karma_pema

can use a wet paper towel or sponge as a base, but the sprouts won't be able to get any traction this way and thus will be very weak. Finally, it's helpful to cover the tray with something, which could be another plastic tray or a cutting board—anything flat that can help keep it from drying out. Otherwise, follow the same basic instructions as the glass jar method for soaking and rinsing. You also can rinse seedling-tray sprouts by spraying them regularly with a spray bottle and dumping out the excess water from the edges. Wheatgrass, which takes a few days longer than eating sprouts, will require some extra nutrition to grow to its full potential. The best growing supplement for any of these methods is kelp extract. Dilute it to a very low strength and spray it on the sprouts to increase their rate of growth and nutritional value.

If you plan to get serious about sprouting, I recommend that you invest between $12 and $250 to buy a sprouting device, which will make the job a lot easier. On the lower end of the scale, the Easy Sprout (available from some of the online retailers listed below) is a small plastic container that maximizes humidity and enables easy rinsing. Another

Delicious bean sprout stir-fry dish. ©iStockphoto.com/susaro

affordable option in tray form is the Back to Basics Kitchen Sprouter, which is normally packed in a kit form that includes some organic alfalfa seed. There are also several mid-sized manual sprouting systems such as the Sproutmaster and Healthy Sprouter, which are larger and slightly more elaborate versions of either a container or a tray.

At the higher end of the price scale are the automatic sprouters, which do the rinsing for you, but do require a little electricity to get the job done. The two main ones on the market are Tribest's Freshlife (about $100, or $150 for an extra growing barrel) and the Easy Green (about $250). Both of these are extremely well-designed commercial-quality sprouters for home gardeners. The Easy Green Sprouter is a flat tray-based system that mists the sprouts regularly to keep them watered, humidified, and oxygenated. It requires an 18" x 24" space, and the unit can both automatically fill and drain the water if it's set up next to a sink. The Freshlife Sprouter has a cylindrical growing barrel that is about 12 inches in diameter. An optional second barrel can be attached on the top to double its growing capacity. The Freshlife automatically maintains humidity levels and a rotating sprinkler rinses the sprouts, but it does not change the water automatically. The downside of this is that you have to change the water yourself once a day or so (which takes about three minutes per day), but the upside is that you can place it anywhere.

The use of automatic sprouters may raise some ethical questions for sustainable gardeners. Are these hydroponic systems? If they use energy and water to get the job done, then how sustainable are they? First, they do qualify as hydroponic systems, but none of them uses lights, so their energy consumption is very low compared to the wasteful systems we associate with the word "hydroponic." The Freshlife, for example, turns on for only a few minutes each hour and it uses just 8 watts of energy, which is much less than a lightbulb. These systems' water use is also quite reasonable. The Easy Green, which is the larger of the two, can produce up to 6 pounds of fresh sprouts each week with only half a gallon of water per day. These systems are far more productive than any hydroponic garden, at a tiny fraction of the energy and water consumption. In fact, with the incredible amounts of water and energy required to farm and transport vegetables and meat, it is very wasteful *not* to have an automatic sprouting system at home that produces your own fresh veggies and protein. In tough times when you may not have energy to cook with, sprouting also gives you a sustainable way to prepare grains and beans for consumption. With no energy available, an automatic sprouter would make a very effective manual sprouter and would simply require occasional rinsing.

What can you grow into sprouts? Here is an incomplete list.

GRAINS: wheat, barley, rye, popcorn, quinoa, and others.

LEGUMES: lentils, peas, adzuki beans, black beans, garbanzo beans, mung beans, soybeans, and others.

GREENS: alfalfa, broccoli, clover, canola, radish, buckwheat, sunflower, and others.

OTHERS: Some people sprout nuts such as almonds and peanuts, micro-greens such as lettuce and arugula, and plants with stronger flavors such as fenugreek and onion.

You can order seeds over the Internet from sprouting seed sources or can simply try your luck in the bulk section of your local health food store. You can mix seeds, but it is usually better to start with separate amounts of each seed type you want to grow, because some take longer to mature than others. Make sure that the seeds are organic or at least untreated. If you are ordering seeds online, then look for ones that are specifically labeled as "sprouting seeds." These should be fresh and have been tested for a high germination rate; they are not always the same seeds that would grow big plants in your garden. Several quality online retailers are the Sprout People (www.sproutpeople.com), with a wealth of information on their Web site; Mumm's Sprouting Seeds (www.sprouting.com); Sunrise Seeds (www.sunriseseeds.com); and Wheatgrass Kits (www.wheatgrasskits.com). Also, try your local health food store's bulk section; you might get lucky and find some good, fresh seeds. I found my best batch of sprouting soybeans this way, which were far more productive for me than any soybeans I have ordered online. The following table gives you some idea of how long it takes for the most common sprouts to mature.

SEED	DAYS
Alfalfa, Broccoli, Radish	5-6 days
Lentils	3-4 days
Mung Beans and Soybeans	4-5 days
Sunflower	7-8 days
Wheat/Wheatgrass	3-4 days/7-10 days

WHEATGRASS JUICE

Wheat, and other cereal grains, grow into grasses, which are not themselves edible but can be juiced to make a nutritious green beverage. Wheat, rye, barley, and triticale all have similar characteristics and can produce juicable grass in around 7 to 10 days. Although you can juice them later than this, the grass is at its nutritional peak at around 7 days, and this will decline as it gets longer and tougher. I have tried sprouting wheat, rye, barley, spelt, and triticale grains for juicing grass. To my taste buds, wheatgrass juice is sweetest of these, ryegrass juice is the most difficult to drink, and the others all taste about the same. Nutritionally, there is not much difference among the cereal grain grasses, but as with any food source, it is good to diversify as much as possible. I usually sprout 80 percent wheatgrass and sow in a handful of barley, rye, or whatever other grains I have on hand. The rye foliage takes on a beautiful dark red or purple tinge, contrasting nicely with the deep green of the wheat. For purposes of this description, I will use the term "wheatgrass" to refer to all of these sprouting cereal grains.

You can grow your own wheatgrass in an automatic sprouter or in a sprouting tray of soil or other medium. I prefer the former, but many people believe that soil provides more nutrients. The truth is that the grain seed has all the nutrients that the grass needs for these first few days of sprouting, though when you rinse the seeds in your sprouter, you can choose to mist them with some seaweed extract or another nutritional source to add some valuable trace minerals and natural growth stimulants. I buy only organic seed, so I know that I am getting not only pesticide-free grain but also hopefully something that has been grown in nutritious soil. As the grass grows, you will need to rinse it very well, and it will become increasingly difficult to keep the grains at the bottom mold-free. It is best not to pack in the wheat grains too tightly when you put them in, allowing some space for the rinsing water to get in between the grains and growing grass. Changing the rinse water frequently is essential. Some of the mail-order Web sites listed above also sell wheatgrass kits, which normally include a sprouting tray and growing medium plus a pound or two of grain seed. This can be a simple way to get started and decide whether sprouting your own wheatgrass is something you want to do on a regular basis.

You also will need a good wheatgrass juicer, either manual or electric. When I first started sprouting, I tried making wheatgrass juice with the electric juicer that we had been using for fruit and vegetable juices. In fact, before I acquired a taste for wheatgrass juice, I used to throw in a few handfuls of the sprouts along with an armful of apples, carrots, and other tasty stuff. To be honest, this juicer did not work all that well for wheatgrass. Though it juiced everything else efficiently, I noticed that I needed a lot of grass sprouts to get any green juice at all. And when I pulled out the blade for cleaning, which was a spinning cylinder that basically looked like a small grater, it had a lot of wheatgrass stuck in it that had not really been juiced. And so I began shopping for a real "wheatgrass juicer." I learned that it is more difficult for most fruit/vegetable juicers to break the cell walls of grass blades and get the juice out, and that some kinds of automatic juicers get hot as they work, which can destroy some of the enzymes in your food. Whether you choose an electric or manual wheatgrass juicer, the best kind is probably a masticating type, which basically makes juice by using a giant drill bit to grind and mash the food between the drill bit and inside of the juicer. If you have ever used or seen a meat grinder, it is practically the same thing with an extra hole and screen that allows juice to separate from the grass pulp. I bought a manual model, which operates with a hand crank and is much more efficient at juicing grass. (It actually does quite well with most fruits and veggies, too, so I can still juice some carrots or apples with my wheatgrass if I want.) This manual juicer is very easy and quick to set up, take down, and wash, which means a lot when you juice frequently. And it feels better, certainly more sustainable, to make one's own juice without electric power. There are a number of good juicers out there, both electric and manual. Do an Internet search for "wheatgrass juicer." You will be surprised at how many retailers sell them and how many different choices you have in a variety of price ranges. Materials and warranties are good indications of a particular juicer's durability. Try to find online consumer reviews of any brands and models that interest you. Happy juicing!

EAT YOUR SPROUTS!

I have a confession to make. Earlier in this book, I made a claim that city residents with an average-sized apartment or condominium can raise up to 10 to 20 percent of their own fresh food. This, I now confess, was a lie. You can actually grow an even *higher* percentage of your own fresh food, depending on what percentage of your diet can consist of fresh sprouts! There is an old saying that "man does not live by bread alone." This is probably true of sprouts also, especially given that you would get weary of eating nothing but sprouts day in and day out (even though, nutritionally, you might meet most of your dietary needs this way). My point is this: If you wanted to grow enough sprouts to live on, using the space in your apartment or condo, you could probably do so. There is simply no other food that you can produce so much of, in so small a space, so quickly, and with such a potent nutritional output. With sprouts, the limiting factor is not space, or light, or soil, or even water. The limiting factor is: How many sprouts can you really eat?

Luckily, I have good news here. There are many different kinds of sprouts, and they are a lot easier to eat than you might think. Sometimes when people visit our home, I show off my automatic sprouter and explain to them how I can grow several pounds of nutritious vegetables every single week. Each time, the houseguests seem suitably impressed. Then they pause politely, and they all ask the same question: What do you do with that many sprouts?

Using sprouts as a major food source is not an integral part of our culinary traditions, though several Asian cultures use bean sprouts as a vegetable. With the exception of wheatgrass sprouts, which are juiced, it is a challenge to incorporate an armload of sprouts into the foods we like to eat, and even tougher to structure a dish around them. Yet pound for pound, sprouts provide more nutrition than many vegetables, are much simpler and quicker to grow, and really do taste great. So it is worthwhile to consider how best to utilize these underrated foods.

We can loosely classify sprouts into three main categories: grain sprouts, bean sprouts, and salad (or sandwich) sprouts. Grains to sprout include wheat, barley, rye, and oats. You can soak these grains and sprout them for just a day or two before eating, in which case they are more of a grain than a vegetable. But as soon as cereal grains sprout into long, green shoots they can no longer be enjoyed as grains, and essentially become more of a grass. Sprouted cereal grasses are normally juiced, since they are too fibrous to digest. Beans, like grains, can be sprouted for a day or two and then eaten as beans. Sprouted lentils and peas are delicious when eaten raw, although I tend to think that cooking improves other types of sprouted beans (though some people like eating all of them raw). Beyond two days, bean sprouts turn into shoots and are grown as protein-rich vegetables. Pea shoots, mung bean sprouts, soybean sprouts, and others can then be harvested after 4 to 6 days of sprouting, and used in many stir-fries, soups, and other dishes. Salad sprouts include all other kinds of sprouting seeds, such as alfalfa, clover, radish, broccoli, sunflower, buckwheat, and more. All of these generally are eaten raw and do not cook well; they taste best enjoyed in salads, sandwiches, and fresh dips.

There are many ways to eat sprouts. For example, I often enjoy eating a raw cereal of sprouted wheat berries with a few sprouted lentils. Sprout the wheat for two days, and rinse the grains before using. Put them in a cereal bowl, pour some milk or soy milk over them, add some fresh fruit if you wish, and enjoy as a sweet, nutty, and nutritionally balanced raw breakfast. My family and I use a lot of mung bean and soybean sprouts in Asian dishes and recipes that we improvise. Salad sprouts add freshness and zest to salads, sandwiches, and dips. You can use alfalfa, clover, or sunflower sprouts as the basis of a salad, and radish or broccoli sprouts provide all the spice you need when chopped and included with yogurt, sour cream, fresh salsa, or bean dips.

What follows are some of my family's favorite sprout recipes. I include these not only because you may enjoy them too, but because they demonstrate some of the diverse uses of sprouts. I hope that you will get some ideas from these and feel confident in creating your own dishes that you and your family will enjoy. Happy sprouting and fresh eating!

SOME SIMPLE RECIPES USING SPROUTS

Vietnamese Sprouted Spring Rolls

This is a great appetizer. You can customize the ingredients depending on availability and preference. Dip the rolls in your favorite sauce, such as Thai hot sauce, hoisin sauce, sweet-and-sour sauce, or salad dressing. For a simple Asian-inspired dipping sauce, combine 1 T cider vinegar or lime juice, 1 T sesame oil, 1 tsp soy sauce, and a few freshly chopped chives. For a peanutty version, substitute salad oil for the sesame oil and then stir in 1 T peanut butter.

> 6 large egg roll wrappers (These are available in Asian grocery stores and many supermarkets. Alternately, you can use large iceberg lettuce or cabbage leaves. The cabbage leaves can be boiled first to make them more flexible.)
> 2 oz. vermicelli or thin rice noodles, cooked according to label directions and drained
> 1 cup alfalfa sprouts, clover sprouts, or baby lettuce leaves
> ½ cup mung bean sprouts (raw or lightly stir-fried, per your preference)
> 1 medium-sized cucumber, grated
> 1 carrot, grated
> 1 bunch cilantro
> 1 handful of fresh mint
> Some different options: ½ avocado, thinly sliced or ½ cup stir-fried tofu, thinly sliced or ½ cup stir-fried shiitake mushrooms or ½ cup coarsely grated red bell pepper

To make the rolls, take out the first egg roll wrapper and dip it in warm water for 30 seconds or until softened. Then lay it out flat on a plate or cookie sheet. Fill it as you would a burrito, leaving a little wrapper space on each end. Place cooked noodles into the wrapper lengthwise from end to end. Then add an equal part of each of the other ingredients, saving a few leaves of mint for a garnish. When it looks full, fold over the two ends of the wrapper. Then fold up the bottom, which should stick to each end, and roll it up to the top of the wrapper. Make sure that it all sticks well. Eat raw with dipping sauce (see instructions above). May also be pan-fried or deep-fried like an egg roll. Garnish with remaining mint leaves or extra cilantro.

Serves 2–3 as an appetizer course.

Sprouted Lentil Burgers

1 cup sprouted lentils (or your favorite sprouted
   beans), sprouted for 3 days.
½ cup chopped walnuts
½ cup cooked brown rice
1 onion, chopped
1 celery stalk, chopped
½ cup red bell pepper, finely chopped
½ cup mung bean sprouts, finely chopped
1 egg or equivalent amount of egg substitute (can be
   omitted, but burgers may be crumbly)
2 T olive oil, plus additional oil to cook the burgers
2 T barbecue sauce
1 tsp herbs (whatever you have on hand: parsley,
   thyme, oregano, marjoram, or rosemary)
Salt and pepper to taste
Option 1: ¼ cup crumbled feta cheese or shredded
   hard cheese (Asiago, Parmesan, or Romano).
Option 2: ¼ cup chopped olives
Option 3: 1 tsp chili peppers, finely chopped, or a few
   shakes of hot sauce

1. Stir-fry onions, celery, red bell pepper, and mung bean sprouts
   in oil until onion is cooked. If any liquid remains, pour out and
   discard. Add herbs and a sprinkle of salt.
2. In a bowl, combine lentils, chopped walnuts, and cooked
   brown rice. Add stir-fried vegetables and stir.
3. Add optional ingredients (cheese, olives, and/or chili peppers)
   and stir. Taste mixture and adjust seasoning to your preference
   by adding more salt, pepper, herbs, or barbecue sauce as
   desired.
4. Add egg and mix thoroughly.
5. Heat oiled skillet to medium-high heat. Form mixture into small
   burgers, flatten as much as possible, and cook on medium high
   heat until bottom side is browned (about 5 minutes). You may

cover pan for part of this time if you want to cook by steaming. Then flip over and cook other side equally, adding more oil to pan if needed.

Makes 12 burgers.

Korean Soybean Sprout-Miso Soup

This is a hybrid version of two traditional Korean soup recipes, using miso and soybean sprouts for the soup base. It goes very well with steamed brown rice. You could also add meat or seafood to the broth if you wish. Miso is a very salty fermented soybean paste that makes a terrific soup base; it is available in Asian grocery stores, health food stores, and many supermarkets. For a thin, mild soup start with 1 T of miso and add more as needed; 3T makes a thicker, saltier stew.

> 8 ounces soybean sprouts, washed and with bean
>   pod skins removed.
> 1–3 T miso
> 7–10 cups water
> 1 zucchini squash, chopped into small cubes
> 1 potato, chopped into small cubes
> ½ package tofu, cut into small cubes
> 1–2 cups chopped napa cabbage, or mustard, turnip
>   or radish greens
> 1 cup sliced mushrooms
> 1 onion, chopped
> 2 scallions, chopped
> 3 cloves garlic, crushed or finely chopped
> Optional: 1 small chili pepper, sliced, or a few shakes
>   of hot sauce

Wash and cut the vegetables, mushrooms, and tofu.

Put 5 cups water in a soup pot on high heat. Add the bean sprouts, cover, and bring to a boil. Turn it down and let this simmer for about 15–20 minutes to create a bean sprout broth.

Stir in the miso.

Add the onion, potato, and mushrooms. Turn the heat up to high again. Let the soup boil for a few minutes.

Add the chopped zucchini, greens, and optional chili pepper. Let it boil a few minutes more, then turn down the heat to a simmer.

Stir the soup and taste it. If it is too thin and bland, add more miso. If it is too strong and salty, add more water.

Add in the chopped scallions and tofu. Cook about three more minutes.

Add the crushed garlic. Stir well, cover, turn off the heat, and let it sit for a few minutes before serving.

Serves 4–6.

Preparing Soybean Sprouts for Stir-fries

Soybean sprouts are tough and need to be cooked before eating. They are delicious in stir-fried side dishes or main courses, but they may take more cooking time to make them soft enough to be edible and digestible. This blanching method both softens the sprouts and removes any bitterness, while the cooked sprouts still taste fresh. If you precook them as directed here, then you can stir-fry the soybean sprouts with anything you wish, including vegetables, noodles, mushrooms, tofu, or the meat of your choice.

8 ounces soybean sprouts, washed and with bean
   pod skins removed
Medium-sized pot of hot water with 2–3 T salt added

Bring the water to a boil.

Add salt and stir.

Add the bean sprouts to boiling water. Let the water boil for another minute and turn it off.

Place pasta strainer in the sink. Pour out the boiling water and sprouts over the strainer.

Cool down the sprouts by running cold water over them.

These blanched sprouts can now be added to any stir-fry dish. They are a great addition to Asian noodle recipes and vegetable side dishes. For a very simple, plain side dish, stir-fry the blanched sprouts with 1 clove crushed garlic, 1 finely chopped scallion, 2 tsp soy sauce, 1 tsp cooking oil, ½ tsp roasted sesame oil, and a handful of sesame seeds. Optional: pinch of crushed red pepper. Withhold the sesame oil and seeds until the end. Cook other ingredients quickly, and add the sesame oil just as you turn off the heat. Sprinkle sesame seeds on top.

Fermented Grainberry Beverage

This recipe is my take on a beverage that is known elsewhere as rejuvelac. Another basic recipe is available from the Sprout People (also a good source of sprout seeds) at www.sproutpeople.com/cookery/rejuvelac.html. If you do not want to use wild yeasts and bacteria to ferment this, you can use some kefir grains. (See the next chapter for more information on this.) This beverage has a somewhat acidic pH and a very low percentage of alcohol (probably less than 1 percent). This recipe makes eight ounces of the drink (just enough for you to try it); if you want to make more, just use more of everything.

> ½ cup grain (wheat, rye, or barley; rye has the best
>   flavor when fermented)
> 8 ounces purified water + rinsing water
> Handful of fresh berries or sliced fruit
> A warm, low-light shelf or other place to put the jar

Rinse the grains and place them in a glass Mason jar, then cover them with lukewarm water. Let them soak for about 8 hours.

Pour out the water. Then rinse the grains again with fresh water. Make sure to pour out as much of the water as possible so that the grains are still wet, but not sitting in water. Then loosely cover the jar with some cloth or the jar lid (just place it on top; do not screw on). Place on a shelf or in a warm location for 10 to 12 hours.

After this time you will notice that the grains have little sprouting "tails," meaning that they have begun their journey from grain to plant. This means that they are chock-full of enzymes and nutrition, much of which will remain in the water that will become your drink.

Rinse again the same way. Then cover grains with 8 ounces of purified or filtered (nonchlorinated) water.

Drop a handful of fresh berries or fruit into the water. My favorite flavors for this drink come from raspberries, apricot, lemon, ginger, and cucumber. Experiment and see what you like.

Cover the jar with the lid, shake it, and let it sit in a warm, dark place for 36 to 48 hours. (Pour out a sip's worth and taste it after 36 hours; let it go longer if you want it more fermented.)

Discard the grains (and compost them) after using.

You have just captured the nutritional essence of spouted grains in this water, which is now full of vitamins, minerals, enzymes, and probiotic microbes. Here, the beneficial bacteria and yeasts come from the grains themselves, though you could also culture this with kefir grains if you prefer. (See the next chapter.)

eight

MAKING YOGURT, KEFIR,
AND FERMENTED FOODS

This is a book about producing food, not cooking or preserving it. Why then, you ask, is there a chapter on fermentation? Fermented foods have a place here because culturing them greatly adds to the nutritive value of the underlying food, as well as enhancing your body's ability to digest and absorb its nutrients. Yogurt, for example, contains around 20 percent more protein than the milk it's made from, and the fermentation process enables your body to more easily absorb its calcium, iron, and amino acids. Fermenting is a way of "growing" or "farming" beneficial microflora that help produce your own superfood. Making yogurt, kefir, sauerkraut, kimchi, or other fermented foods is a simple activity that is fun, quick, and brings enormous nutritional benefits to you and your family. Best of all, you can ferment these foods just about anywhere: a dark cupboard, shelf, countertop, oven rack, stairwell, back porch, garage, or storage locker can work quite well.

From Armenian *mazun* to Zambian *munkoyo*, there are more than one thousand traditional fermented foods in the world, and these include various alcoholic drinks, dairy foods, fish, vegetables, fruit, beans, meat, grains, pastes, and sauces. Here we will focus on four simple and nutritious ones that you can make easily at home: yogurt, kefir, sauerkraut, and kimchi. The first of these, yogurt, is probably the most familiar to readers. Yogurt is produced by inoculating milk with a starter culture that includes one or more strains of friendly bacteria. These bacteria feed on the lactose in milk, causing the liquid to curdle into a more solid, custardy food with a pudding texture and a lightly sour taste. Yogurt tastes delicious with fresh fruit, in cereal, or blended into a smoothie. You can also make yogurt from goat or sheep's milk, or even from other types of nondairy "milk," including soy milk, coconut milk, almond milk, and rice milk.

Kefir is closely related to yogurt, but with even stronger healthful properties. The term *kefir* is a Turkish word that loosely translates to "feel good" in English. Although you can buy a commercial product labeled as "kefir" in some health food stores, this is basically a cultured milk drink that does not use actual kefir starter. True kefir can be made only with a culture of kefir grains, which are small colonies of friendly bacteria and yeasts. All kefir grains come from an original mother culture with very ancient origins.[61] The grains were first used many centuries ago in the Caucasus region of Central Asia, where residents still consider kefir an important food staple, and where they enjoy some of the longest life expectancies in the world. According to one story, the prophet Mohammed made a gift of kefir grains to the people of this region, and they became a closely guarded secret throughout the ages.[62] Despite a healthy track record that probably spans thousands of years, modern scientific research has only begun to scratch the surface with kefir, confirming that its constituent organisms are an extremely symbiotic community of yeasts and bacteria that exhibit strong probiotic qualities and are capable of beneficially colonizing the human gastrointestinal tract.[63] Kefir grains can be used to culture milk, vegetables, fruit juice, and sugar water. Remarkably, the very same grains also can culture and create just about any fermented food, including a delicious sourdough bread, ginger beer, sauerkraut, or kimchi.

Sauerkraut and kimchi are both fermented vegetable dishes with a pickley taste; the fermentation process effectively preserves the nutrients in the vegetables for a period of several months. Sauerkraut is a fermented cabbage dish that is traditional in Germany and Eastern Europe, and Korean kimchi is an ever-present side dish in that country that is most commonly made with fermented cabbage, daikon radish, or cucumber. No special culture is needed for either preparation, since they are fermented by naturally occurring lactic acid bacteria—though a starter is sometimes used in traditional recipes. For sauerkraut and water-based kimchi, shredded cabbage is submerged in a salty brine and left to ferment, but most kinds of kimchi use a paste of crushed red pepper, garlic, and salt to cover the fermenting vegetables. Sauerkraut and kimchi both contain high levels of vitamins A, B, and C, as well as boasting more friendly bacteria than yogurt. Kimchi, with a greater diversity of vegetable ingredients, was chosen in 2006 as one of the five "World's Healthiest Foods" by *Health* magazine, which touted its benefits for digestion, cancer prevention, and immunity against yeast infections.[64]

MAKING YOGURT

To make yogurt, you just need some milk and yogurt culture, as well as a container, mixing spoon, and an optional bowl for mixing. The container can be a glass jar, ceramic bowl, or any nonmetallic vessel. Containers and utensils should be sterilized or at least thoroughly washed before beginning, and the milk should be at room temperature or a little warmer. If you heat the milk to a boil first and then allow it to cool to room temperature, this will ensure a thicker yogurt. If you use soy milk, which does not contain lactose, then it's necessary to add a spoonful or two of sugar or maple syrup to encourage the bacteria.

To the room-temperature milk or soy milk, you then add the starter culture, which can be either freeze-dried yogurt starter or a good-quality commercial yogurt. If you use a commercial yogurt as a starter, then you need to follow some important guidelines in selecting it. First, buy the plain stuff (no flavors, no sugars, and no colors added). Second, you need to use yogurt with "active cultures," which should be noted on the container. If there are no active/live cultures, or if it has been pasteurized *after* the yogurt fermentation, then the stuff is useless as a starter. Some yogurt containers use the words "cultures added after pasteurization," but in lieu of this additional information, you may just have to experiment and find out which type works best. Third, I would avoid any yogurt that has added pectin or another thickener listed as an ingredient, since this is evidence that it is not all that pure and its cultures were not potent enough to do the job on their own. Fourth, consider that more bacterial diversity is probably a good thing; many yogurts are made with no more than three or four cultures (generally *L. acidophilus*, *S. thermophilus*, *L. bulgaricus*, and/or *L. bifidus*), although a few health-oriented brands also use other *Lactobacillus* species such as *L. casei*, *L. reuteri*, and/or *L. rhamnosus*. Studies have proven that each of these additional species provides numerous benefits as probiotics and/or immune system enhancers.[65] Also, the more commonly used *S. thermophilus*, and *L. bulgaricus* do not survive the gastrointestinal journey in high enough numbers to colonize your digestive tract.[66] Fifth, try to buy organic yogurt if it's available, since you know your starter culture will be free of pesticides, hormones, steroids, and whatever else they feed big-dairy cows these days. This is an even more important consideration for the milk you buy to make your yogurt. For my money, the best commercial yogurts to use for starter cultures are made by Nancy's Yogurt, Stonyfield Farms, and Horizon Organic Dairy, but you may find a favorite local or regional brand in your area. Organic milks have become available in many supermarkets over the past few years. However, you should know that milk that is labeled "ultra-pasteurized," "UHT," or "shelf stable" has been heated to a point that changes the molecular composition; such milk will not culture into yogurt very well because the microbial enzymes are less effective at breaking it down. If I walked into a store and the only organic milk they had was ultra-pasteurized, I would buy some non-organic milk instead for making yogurt.

If using dried starter, follow the package directions. If using commercial yogurt as a starter, then mix in approximately one part yogurt to six parts milk. Yogurt should be heated to slightly above typical room temperature (70 degrees F, or 21 degrees C) to accelerate its biological activity, though a weaker yogurt can be made at room temperature. You can warm it in an oven or on top of a heating pad that does not get the mixture much hotter than lukewarm. Temperatures above 112 degrees F can kill the good bacteria, so if your oven or heating pad gets hotter than this, it will start to cook the milk instead of fermenting it. The proper fermentation time depends on whether you like a mild, drinkable yogurt (as little as 3 to 4 hours) or a dense, sour yogurt (7 to 8 hours or longer), and it depends a little on the air temperature as well. I find that the strength of the starter culture also plays a big part in fermentation time, and this can vary greatly.

The lazy (and most reliable) way to make yogurt is to buy a yogurt maker, which is essentially an electric warming device that keeps the mixture at an optimum temperature for yogurt formation (between

Kefir grains. ©iStockphoto.com/esemelwe

about 108 and 112 degrees F). Yogurt is delicious eaten plain or with some maple syrup, honey, fresh fruit, sprouted wheat berries, granola, or other cereal. Remember to save a few ounces of your yogurt to use as starter culture for the next batch!

MAKING MILK-BASED AND WATER-BASED KEFIR

Kefir is probably the parent of all yogurts. You can make it only using live or freeze-dried kefir grains, which are lumpy colonies of probiotic bacteria and yeasts. (The milk-based ones look like wet popcorn puffs.) All of these stem from an original mother culture, so you must obtain them from someone who cultures kefir. High-quality dried kefir starter can be ordered from the Body Ecology online store (www.shop.bodyecology.com) or Yogurt For Life (www.yogurtforlife.com). Live kefir grains are available from a few retail sources and individual sellers on the Internet. Four of these, which I have not tried and cannot

Soymilk kefir fermenting in a clay pot (left). Yogurt jars in a yogurt maker (right).

vouch for personally, are www.anahatabalance.com, www.wilderness familynaturals.com, www.gemcultures.com, and www.bacteriapimp .com/store. Also, there are active kefir sellers and traders on eBay and in Yahoo Groups. You could also check with your local health food store.

Kefir is cultured at room temperature for about 24 to 48 hours. You can make it in any nonmetallic container, such as a glass jar or clay crock. You will also need a strainer (preferably plastic rather than metal), a nonmetallic spoon, and another container to store the finished kefir in the refrigerator. Everything should be thoroughly washed prior to use. Since kefir grains are sensitive to ultraviolet (UV) light, it is best to put the kefir container in a cabinet, unused oven, or other dark place. To get started, fill the jar about three-fourths full with milk. If you are using dried kefir culture, follow the directions on the box. If you have live kefir grains as your culture, then gently drop a spoonful or two into the milk. One tablespoon will culture about 8 to 16 ounces of milk; using more may increase the sourness. Cover the container loosely with a lid or towel. In 24 hours, the kefir will be a thin, mild beverage with a sourdough-like taste that is similar to yogurt. For a thick, sour kefir, allow it to ferment for 48 hours at room temperature. Using a yogurt maker or warm oven to accelerate the biological activity is not recommended with kefir, as it can throw off the natural balance of the organisms.

When the kefir is sour enough for your taste, it is time to strain out the grains from the kefir liquid. Using a strainer over another container or glass, pour out the kefir and make sure that all the grains have reached the strainer. These grains can be placed immediately into some new milk for the next batch of kefir. If you want to store them instead, put them in a covered cup of milk in the refrigerator, and continue to refresh the milk every few days. They will stay fresh this way for up to two weeks. If you keep these grains alive and well fed, either through continuous use or by alternating storage and use, then you will never again need to buy new kefir culture.

Kefir grains can be used to culture goat's milk, soy milk, fruit juice, and sugar water as well. For soy milk or goat's milk, just follow the same directions as for regular milk, but make sure to add a teaspoon or so of sugar, molasses, or maple syrup to the soy milk, just as you would in making soy yogurt. Honey has a mild antibiotic effect due to plant resins that the bees collect, so it is not ideal for fermentation use. (If you like the taste and health benefits of honey, you could certainly sweeten your yogurt with it after fermentation.)

If you want to make juice- or water-based kefir, then you should obtain some kefir grains that have been developed for this purpose. So-called "water kefir" grains are widely available from the sources listed above, and they will ferment effectively using plant sugars rather than the sugars found in milk. You can make a great brewed soda pop or ginger beer using a tablespoon of kefir grains in sixteen ounces of filtered (chlorine-free) water in a jar. As a general rule, I use about the same amount of sweetener as kefir grains, so a tablespoon or so of sugar, maple syrup, or molasses will suffice. Adding a pinch each of sea salt and baking soda will ensure that the organisms also have some mineralization. Finally, I cut in some fresh, peeled ginger slices and/or a little fruit for flavor. A slice of apricot, peach, fig, lemon, cucumber, or a couple of berries add

Making yogurt cheese using a coffee filter, strainer, and glass pitcher. Over a day or two, the whey liquid will separate and drain to the bottom, leaving a rich and healthy cream cheese/sour cream substitute on top.

a great flavor twist. To keep the kefir grains pure, you can suspend your fruit or ginger in the water using a cloth bag or unbleached coffee filter. Before setting the jar to ferment, lightly shake it so that a few oxygen bubbles get into the water. For a naturally carbonated, champagne-like beverage, close the lid tightly. For no carbonation, cover the jar loosely. Let it sit for 24 hours, or up to 48 hours for a sour version. For a slightly (1 to 3 percent) alcoholic drink, use extra sugar, keep the lid on tightly, let it ferment for about 48 hours in a warm, dark place, and lightly shake it a few times during this period. If the taste is too sour for you, add a little sugar before you drink it. To reduce the alcohol content of kefir, keep the lid covered very loosely and do not shake during fermentation. The regular alcohol content of water kefir is less than 0.5 percent (milk kefir is lower still), and for those concerned about children consuming kefir, this has been a common practice for many hundreds (probably thousands) of years in Central Asia, with no ill effects.

Making Yogurt or Kefir Cheese

You can make a spreadable cheese (resembling cream cheese or sour cream) from either yogurt or kefir. You will notice that when you make either yogurt or kefir, it becomes more solid and sour the longer you let it ferment. Make sure to start the cheese with some mature yogurt or kefir, not the particularly runny stuff; give it a few extra hours of fermentation time for good measure.

> A few ounces of strong yogurt or kefir
> Large glass jar, measuring beaker, bowl, or clay pot
> One square of cheesecloth or large coffee filter
> Strainer that fits over this container or an extra-large
>   piece of cheesecloth
> Large rubber band or twine

Wrap your homemade yogurt in cheesecloth or a coffee filter. Using the strainer or extra cheesecloth (with rubber band or twine if needed), suspend this package above the container. Make sure it has room to drip. Put this in the refrigerator, an unused oven, or anywhere else it will fit and be relatively undisturbed. Leave and allow it to drain for 24 to 48 hours. Your main goal here is to strain out the water (whey) from the yogurt or kefir, leaving a solid mass that can be used like cheese. This recipe makes a nutritious, low-fat cheese.[67] Be aware that your yogurt or kefir will continue to ferment during this time, so if you want a milder version, then you might want to put the cheese into the refrigerator as it drains. (This will slow down the fermentation.) Use the finished product as you would use cream cheese or sour cream. And don't forget the whey: this liquid byproduct makes a refreshing drink on its own, or, if coming from kefir, it could be used to culture a batch of kimchi or sourdough starter.

Making Sauerkraut

The word *sauerkraut* means "sour cabbage" in German, and this is an accurate description for this fermented dish. It is very simple to make. Start with a head of cabbage, some sea salt, a mixing bowl, and a lidded jar. You can also use any other nonmetallic container. Traditionally, sauerkraut is made in a large clay fermenting crock. One important note on ingredients: Please use organic cabbage and natural sea salt. Pesticide residues and the iodine in table salt are both artificial and can interfere with the biological activity in sauerkraut production. Sea salt also adds a range of trace minerals, which will assist the fermentation.

1. Wash the head of cabbage and shred it. You can use a food processor, hand grater or mandolin, or just chop it into thin shreds. Put shredded cabbage in the mixing bowl.

2. Cover the cabbage with 1 to 2 tablespoons of salt, and use your hands (they should be clean) to mix it in. Squeeze the cabbage lightly to release some of its juice.

3. Put it in the container and cover it. After one day, if there is not enough liquid to cover the cabbage, add a little water.

4. The sauerkraut will begin fermenting quickly, and in warmer weather, may be ready for you to eat in a matter of days. Check it daily, taste a small spoonful, and when you find it tangy enough for your tastes, move the whole container to the refrigerator to slow down its development. Alternately, you may decide to eat it in different stages of development, taking out a small portion every day or so until it is heavily fermented. In cooler temperatures, sauerkraut can keep fermenting for months. Some freeze or can it once it is ready to eat, while others make smaller batches for fresh eating on a regular basis.

5. Sauerkraut uses an anaerobic fermentation process under the salt water, so if this evaporates, feel free to add more water anytime. If the cabbage is above the water for any period of time, you may see some mold from airborne organisms. Scrape this off as best you can, making sure that the remainder of the sauerkraut is packed in below water level.

6. You can use sauerkraut as a condiment on sandwiches or a side dish with just about any meal. If your sauerkraut is tangy enough, you also can use it as the basis for a sauce or marinade. Try combining a cup of sauerkraut or sauerkraut juice with ¼ cup each of fruit juice and olive oil. Add in a crushed clove or two of garlic, a smaller amount of mustard or ginger, and a small handful of fresh herbs. Feel free to adjust the ingredients to your liking.

MAKING KIMCHI

Kimchi is Korea's signature side dish, present in at least one form at every meal. Chock-full of fresh vegetables, vitamins, good bacteria, and enzymes, it is one of the healthiest things you can put in your body.

A traditional Korean radish kimchi, made with small, whole daikon radishes, including the greens.

There are hundreds of different varieties of kimchi, using all manner and combinations of fermented vegetables and other foods, but the most common kimchis are based on napa cabbage, radish, or cucumber, with a pasty sauce of crushed chili pepper, garlic, and salt. In this section, you will learn three simple kimchi recipes; feel free to improvise and repeat the basic technique with your favorite vegetables. If the spicy taste of crushed red chili and garlic is too strong for you, feel free to reduce these ingredients to fit your palate. A chili-free version of the following dish is called "white kimchi" and tastes much like sauerkraut. Kimchi is briefly ripened at room temperature and then moved to the refrigerator, but in cool temperatures it could be stored outside.

Napa Cabbage Kimchi

Kimchi, like sauerkraut, is fermented traditionally in large clay pots. You also can use a glass jar or any nonmetallic container, and this recipe also will require two mixing bowls (one large, one small). You will need:

> 1 napa cabbage, preferably organic
> 4 tablespoons sea salt
> 2 3 green onions or scallions
> 1 clove garlic, minced or crushed
> 2/3 cup hot red pepper powder
> 1/4 teaspoon ginger, crushed or grated
> 1/2 tablespoon sugar
> Optional: 1 tablespoon of water kefir, fermented
>   shrimp paste, or other source of live culture, which
>   will accelerate the fermentation.

1. Wash the napa cabbage well, discarding the outer leaves.
2. Chop the leaves. Their size should be similar to chopped lettuce in a typical salad.
3. Put the chopped cabbage in the large bowl. Sprinkle in a little sea salt, rub it into the leaves, and mix together.
4. In the smaller bowl, mix the crushed garlic, red pepper powder,

ginger, sugar, remaining salt, and optional culture. This should form a pasty sauce. Add a spoonful or two of nonchlorinated water if it seems too dry.

5. Pour the sauce paste over the chopped cabbage. Add the chopped green onion. Toss gently until it is coated.

6. Place the whole mixture in a glass jar or other container. Cover it loosely with the lid or a cloth. Once the kimchi begins to give off a fermenting smell (which could be in a few hours or a day or two, depending on the climate/temperature), fasten the lid tightly and put the jar in the refrigerator to slow down the fermentation. Your kimchi is now ready to eat. It can be stored in the refrigerator for up to several months, but will begin to taste progressively stronger. If you like a fresher taste, eat it quickly. If you do not mind a sour kimchi, then allow it to continue ripening. Ripened kimchi, when chopped, can add incredible flavoring to fried rice, stir-fried noodles, or stew.

Radish Kimchi

This is made just like the cabbage kimchi above, except with daikon radish cubes as the main ingredient. Use one large daikon radish, which should be thoroughly washed and peeled (an alternate version uses roughly the same quantity of baby daikon radishes, which are fermented whole, roots and greens, without chopping them). You will use the same ingredients as above, plus ½ tablespoon of grated fresh ginger (more if you really like ginger). Again, the culture from kefir water or fermented shrimp is optional, but will speed things up.

1. Chop the peeled radish into cubes. In a mixing bowl, add some of the salt and begin to rub it in.

2. In the smaller bowl, mix together the remainder of the salt plus other sauce ingredients as in the previous recipe.

3. Pour sauce mixture over cubed radish, add in chopped green onion, and stir until well coated. Transfer kimchi mixture into a

jar or other container, cover loosely, and allow it to ferment as described in the napa kimchi recipe.

4. Older radish kimchi, which has a stronger fermented flavor, makes an incredible base for soups and stews.

Water Kimchi

Water kimchi is a soupier version in which both the vegetables and their broth get fermented deliciously. If you like the taste of pickles, this is a good one to try. Start with a few leaves of napa cabbage, washed and chopped like salad lettuce. A small daikon radish, washed and peeled, should be cut lengthwise into quarters and then sliced. Other optional ingredients include sliced pear, apple, or pickling cucumber. For additional twists, you can add sliced jujubes (the shriveled red dates found in Asian markets) or a few sprigs of parsley or watercress. The remainder of the ingredients and directions are the same as for the recipes above, except that once you mix things together, you will cover the kimchi with nonchlorinated water plus enough extra salt to suit your taste buds. Put this mixture in a loosely covered jar or other container, and allow it to ferment for about 24 hours. At this point, you can store it in the refrigerator and start eating it; water kimchi is served in a small bowl and eaten like a cold soup. Pear and apple slices will ferment more quickly than the veggies, so you can pick these out and eat them sooner, as the fermentation will continue slowly even in the refrigerator. One warning: Water kimchi is very aromatic! In my family, we have a separate small refrigerator for fermented foods, and I am told that in Korea a separate kimchi refrigerator is now a standard home appliance.

WILD ABOUT FERMENTATION?

You may find yourself becoming addicted to the process of fermenting foods. Unless you are consuming too much of your own moonshine or other inebriating substance, then home fermentation is a healthful preoccupation to have. Once you've developed more than a passing interest in fermentation, you owe yourself a small present that will really expand your understanding of its vital place in our lives. The book *Wild Fermentation* by Sandor Ellix Katz is a much-needed addition to your library. It is a practical guide to preparing fermented foods and an exploration of life through the author's passion for wild fermentation in a world of antibiotics and antibacterial soaps. Mr. Katz presents the process of food fermentation as an age-old tradition that has been central to numerous cultures around the world. He honors these traditions in sharing their recipes, while also presenting fresh innovations involving homemade misos, sauerkrauts, kimchis, tempehs, chutneys, sourdough cultures, wines, vinegars, and much more. This book would be a featured selection in my book club if I had one, and I highly recommend it to all readers.[68]

nine

CULTIVATING MUSHROOMS

One way to use darker spaces, including those in shady yards or unused garage areas, is to grow mushrooms. Cultivating mushrooms can provide you with a delicious supplemental food source, and over time this could even grow into a supplemental income. Mushrooms contain protein, are full of minerals, and certain varieties are credited with tremendous health benefits in the Chinese/Oriental and Ayurvedic systems of medicine. Moreover, gourmet mushrooms are expensive in markets and restaurants, enough so that you may decide to grow a few extra for trade or sale. More than a few amateur mushroom growers have turned this hobby into a business after a few years of growing and learning.

Mushrooms are classified as fungi, and the mushroom buttons we eat are actually the floral blooms of these fungi. Mushroom caps release powdery spores into the air, which colonize growing areas with mycelium. Mycelium appears as a fuzzy moldlike growth, which contains many tiny strands of the fungus. In this form, they can grow in a substrate material such as wood, hay, or compost, until they once again bloom. There are more than 200 types of edible mushrooms, but home mushroom growers usually focus on a handful of species that grow dependably from cultivation.

It is simple to grow mushrooms on a small scale, but more challenging to grow more of them at a lower cost. There are basically two levels of mushroom growers: beginner hobbyists and more experienced cultivators. Everyone starts out as a hobbyist, but unfortunately the mushrooms you produce this way will not justify the cost of getting started. Luckily, if you stick with this pursuit, you can reuse some of your initial ingredients to continue producing mushrooms over a longer period without much added expense. Transitioning to this larger-scale production brings down the cost of your mushrooms considerably. You also will learn a lot from small-scale growing, and in future this experience will help you produce more mushrooms in less time for fewer dollars, which makes this a very rewarding food production scheme in the long run. For larger-scale mushroom growing, you will need some space where you can keep damp wood logs, sawdust, or straw, which could be a garage or a shady patch in the yard.

Most amateur mushroom growers begin with a prepackaged growing kit, which generally consists of a growth medium (such as a jar with sawdust, a box of sterile compost, or a drilled piece of wood), mushroom spores (called spawn), detailed instructions, and perhaps a few other odds and ends. This is the best way to learn how mushrooms grow in your particular climate and conditions, and you will be able to reuse the spores later on. Although you could start on a larger scale right away, you also stand to suffer greater losses this way without the benefit of experience. Some widely used Internet and mail-order suppliers of kits and spawn include Mushroom People (www.mushroompeople.com), Gourmet Mushrooms (www.gmushrooms.com), Fungi Perfecti (www.fungi.com), Field and Forest Products (www.fieldforest.net), Gardener's Supply (www.gardeners.com), and the UK-based Organic Mushroom Company (www.gourmetmushrooms.co.uk). The most easily cultivated home mushroom varieties are oysters, shiitakes, white buttons, and criminis/portabellas, roughly in that order. Once you get the hang of growing a simpler variety, you can try more delicate and exotic varieties such as winecaps, cinnamon caps, morels, enokis, and reishis.

The first important step is to obtain some spores (spawn) from a reputable source, such as one of the suppliers just listed. If you start with a kit, then it will come with growing directions. If you prefer to prepare your own growing medium instead, you still will need to order spores. The right growing medium depends on the type of mushroom you choose, so you should determine the growing requirements for any spore before ordering. If you plan to grow mushrooms in particularly hot or cold conditions, then check with spore or kit suppliers to make sure the strains they offer will fruit in your weather. Fungi feed on the carboneous material found in organic matter. Many woodland and shelf-type mushrooms prefer to grow in wood, so the best growing medium

Oyster mushrooms are easy to grow indoors. ©iStockphoto.com/luriete

for these fungi are hardwood logs, but sawdust is another possibility for raising some wood mushrooms. Sawdust from logs is preferable to sawdust from lumber, both because it is closer to the proper moisture content and because it is untreated. Other types grow well on a grain-based substrate that is usually some mix of soaked whole grains and sawdust. And then there are compost mushrooms, which like to grow and bloom in partly decomposed organic matter such as half-finished compost. This should not be surprising, since fungi often team with earthworms and microbes to decompose organic matter and make its nutrients available for plant growth. Remembering their place in the world may make it easier to cultivate mushrooms! Here are some tips on how to cultivate two common mushroom varieties that are delicious in many cooked dishes, simple to grow, and good fits for many urban-sized spaces.

GROWING OYSTER MUSHROOMS INDOORS

Oyster mushrooms are probably the easiest kind of mushrooms to grow. Though they are accustomed naturally to growing in wood, you also can raise oyster mushrooms in a variety of other growing media, including straw or sawdust. The easiest way to begin is with a kit. If you want to experiment on your own, then oysters give you a greater chance of success than other mushrooms. There are dozens of varieties of oyster mushrooms, from pin-sized to trumpet-sized, so check with your kit or spore supplier to see which kinds are available and recommended for your climate. Most grow in an ideal temperature range of about 55 to 65 degrees F.

Most oyster mushroom growing kits consist of either a small inoculated log or a holey plastic bag filled with sterilized, inoculated straw or sawdust. You can make your own kit using any of these materials, but I will recommend one other method that has worked well for many indoor mushroom growers. For this you will need two milk cartons or small waxed-cardboard boxes, enough sawdust to fill them, 2 cups of whole grain flour or coffee grounds, and some oyster mushroom spawn. The basic steps are as follows, but feel free to improvise. If sawdust is unavailable, you could also use straw for this.

1. Cut out the top of the milk cartons so that their edges are of even height. Punch several small holes in each side of both cartons.

2. Sterilizing (optional): If you are using sawdust that has already been inoculated with spawn, then do not try to sterilize it or you will kill the fungi. If you are using additional sawdust that has not been inoculated yet, then you may want to sterilize it. The easiest ways to do this are by boiling, steaming, or microwaving it. If anyone else in your household might object to cooking sawdust in the kitchen, then you might want to try this step when no one else is home. To sterilize with a microwave oven, fill a microwave-safe bowl with sawdust, plus the flour or coffee grounds, and wet down this mass with enough water so that it is the consistency of

Shiitake mushrooms growing on a log. ©iStockphoto.com/otoFoto

a wet sponge. You may need to do several successive batches to sterilize all of your sawdust. Nuking the sawdust on high for two minutes or until the water begins to boil off will kill any unwanted organisms and leave your kitchen smelling like either a wood shop or coffee shop. You also can boil or steam the growing medium in a pot of water in the kitchen or over a campfire, with or without a steamer basket. After it has boiled for a few minutes, turn off the heat, keep the sawdust covered, and let it return to room temperature.

3. Using nonchlorinated water, wet the sawdust until it's thoroughly damp. Then mix in your spores or inoculated material.

4. Tightly pack this damp growing medium into your milk cartons and leave them in a cellar, garage, storage locker, or dark cabinet. You can put some plastic underneath the cartons and cover them loosely with plastic if desired. If insects are a problem, then spray cooking oil around the plastic to trap them. Keep the sawdust mix moistened regularly with nonchlorinated water, and in a few months your fungi should fruit repeatedly. To harvest mushrooms, twist them out gently so that their stems do not break.

GROWING SHIITAKE MUSHROOMS IN A GARAGE OR YARD

Some of the most expensive and delicious gourmet mushrooms on the market are shiitakes, which also are credited in Asia with healthful properties such as lowering cholesterol and improving immunity to cancer. They are simple to grow in logs and take about 6 to 18 months to emerge. They can fruit in a wide range of temperatures, from just above freezing to nearly 90 degrees F. To grow shiitake mushrooms on logs, the process is as follows. You will need some hardwood logs (such as oak or beech) about 4 to 6 inches in diameter, a strong drill, shiitake spawn (preferably a strain that is suitable for your growing area; check with the supplier for more info), a hammer, and some hot wax (such as cheese wax or candle wax) that can be melted to seal in the spawn.

1. Obtain hardwood logs. Logs that were cut recently are best, but let fresh wood sit at least six weeks before using. Leave the bark on if possible.
2. Drill rings of holes in the log 1 inch deep. Space the holes about 6 inches apart and space the rings about 1½ to 2 inches apart. If possible, alternate the holes in equal spaces and with a zigzag pattern.
3. Into these holes, insert the shiitake spawn. You can order this from suppliers in three forms: inoculated wooden

dowels, loose sawdust, or pressurized sawdust pellets. If you get them in dowel form, pound these into the drilled holes with a hammer. Otherwise, insert the sawdust spawn into the holes.

4. Most people like to seal in the spawn with hot wax, which provides a sterilized outer edge and prevents insects or animals from interfering during the incubation period.

5. The mycelium typically will take 6 to 18 months to grow out through the wood. During this time, you can store the logs in a plastic bag in the garage or on the ground outside, covered loosely with a plastic tarp. Make sure to punch a few holes in any plastic covering you use to allow for adequate airflow.

6. Keep the log moist by watering when necessary with nonchlorinated water. Under ideal conditions, the plastic will help maintain humidity, but during dry spells, you should water gently as often as twice per week. Other types of log-raised mushrooms need direct contact with soil (via a partially buried log), but shiitakes do not.

7. The shiitakes will continue to bloom regularly for 4 to 5 years from the same logs. They will appear on their own schedule, but always remember to keep the logs a little moist. One secret to triggering a bloom (after the first bloom cycle) is to soak the log in ice water every two months or so. Mushrooms will appear within a week or so following the ice water treatment. You may want to alternate which log you soak so that they do not all bloom at once.

I believe anyone can be successful with mushroom cultivating at a basic level, but if you want to grow specialty varieties or turn this into a commercial pursuit, then you have a lot more to learn. Like any complex undertaking, you will need to research it well, read some books, network with a local group of mushroom enthusiasts, and learn through your own experimentation. I hesitate to recommend any books for beginning mushroom growers because I have not found any that are truly appropriate, but Paul Stamets's books are probably as close as you can get. Though they are accessible for any level of learner, Stamets's books are a strong initiation to the methods and terminology of serious mushroom cultivation, so you will not remain a beginner for long. For more information, check out *Growing Gourmet and Medicinal Mushrooms* or *The Mushroom Cultivator: A Practical Guide to Growing Mushrooms at Home*, both by this author. [69]

ten

RAISING CHICKENS AND HONEYBEES IN THE CITY

If you like to eat fresh eggs or honey, consider raising your own chickens or bees in the city. A chicken coop can fit in a lot of urban spaces, even some where food plants cannot be grown, and a few hens can give you dozens of fresh eggs every week. A mobile chicken coop, sometimes known as a "chicken tractor," can be moved around one's backyard or garden so that the birds can eat all the pests and weed seeds in one area, fertilize the soil with their droppings, and then be moved to the next spot. Beehives do not require much horizontal space either, and the benefits are plenty—your own fresh honey as well as bees to pollinate all the crops in your neighborhood.

CHICKENS

Most people who keep chickens raise them for eggs. This is sustainable farming at its best. Chickens can roam a small backyard and rid it of insects, slugs, and weed seeds. In exchange, you can get around 4 to 7 eggs per week from each chicken plus some yard fertilizer. Free-range chicken eggs are delicious and nutritious; if you've never had fresh eggs, you'll be amazed at how much better they taste than the factory-farmed ones. If you have access only to a shared yard or common area in an apartment or condominium building, you might try talking your neighbors and building management into sharing some chickens. If you volunteer to take care of the birds, others might agree to share the small costs in exchange for some eggs, and this could give you access to the yard space. If allowing chickens to roam is impossible where you live, then look into buying or building a chicken tractor, which is essentially

Raise your own chickens in a small space and have fresh eggs every week. ©iStockphoto.com/joanek

a mobile pen that you can wheel from place to place. Using a chicken tractor allows the birds to eat all the bugs, seeds, and weeds they want in one spot and then move to another. If you live in a larger building with a shared backyard, tell your building manager or homeowners' association that your chickens can fertilize the lawn. For more information on chicken tractors and various plans for building your own, take a look at the book *Chicken Tractor: A Permaculture Guide to Happy Hens and Healthy Soil*.[70] If you don't have any space to let chickens roam, then you can still keep them in a small coop, but you'll have to provide all their food, and this can get more expensive.

Before deciding to get chickens, make sure that it's legal to keep them where you live. Many cities or counties regulate chicken raising through local zoning ordinances. You can find out what these laws are by visiting the Web site for your local city or county. (If you live in an incorporated city, check both the city and county laws to be safe.) On the website, look for a link to "Ordinances" or "Code." If you can't find these and the search function does not help, then go to your local public library and ask the librarian for a copy of the ordinances. The good news is that even though many cities regulate chickens, most of them do permit you to keep a few chickens for personal use.

For example, in Seattle, Washington, the city's Municipal Code allows residents to keep up to three "domestic fowl" on any lot. If the lot exceeds a certain square footage, then additional fowl are permitted. St. Louis, Missouri, allows up to four total domestic animals (including chickens) to be kept "as pets" on any parcel. In Miami, Florida, a resident can keep up to 15 hens or 30 growing chicks at any time, but no roosters, and these birds must be kept at least 100 feet from any neighbor's home. Chicago, Illinois, has no limit on the number of chickens permitted for eggs, but they may not be raised for slaughter. Cedar City, Utah, requires residents to apply for a Board of Health permit in order to raise up to 25 chickens, pigeons, ducks, or turkeys. In Minneapolis, Minnesota, a permit is also required, which the commissioner of health will issue only if 80 percent of your neighbors within 100 feet give their consent. In Riverside, California, roosters and other "crowing fowl" are not permitted in general residential zones, but residents can keep up to five chickens or pigeons as long as they are penned or cooped up a certain distance from any residence on an adjacent lot. Vancouver, British Columbia, and East Lansing, Michigan, do not allow any poultry or livestock to be kept. An old New York City ordinance only allows apartment dwellers to keep "Antwerp or homing pigeons" but not other poultry. These examples give you some idea of the wide range of rules that exist out there.

Even if it is legal to keep chickens where you live, you can still run afoul of other laws relating to public health and noise levels. Public health laws remind you to keep the pens clean and the chickens free from disease, which is a good idea anyway. Keep an eye on the news regarding the spread of poultry diseases such as the avian flu. If such diseases proliferate in coming years, governments may develop new controls to limit the proximity of chickens to humans. Also, if a major disease problem arises, the federal government's National Animal Identification System (NAIS) could become mandatory, rather than voluntary in certain states or for certain types of animals. Where noise ordinances are in force, residents may be cited or fined for animals that bother the neighbors. Hens are not as loud as roosters, but they can cluck enough to bother close neighbors. One way to handle this is to talk to your neighbors before getting the chickens and help them understand what you are planning. (*Hint:* If you offer neighbors some free eggs, they may see the logic in your plans.)

If you are renting your home, don't forget that keeping "pets" of any sort may violate your lease agreement. Read your lease and check with the property owner if you're unsure; he or she might agree to some outdoor chickens if they agree that the lease was written to prevent indoor dogs and cats. Again, assuring an owner of cleanliness and offering fresh eggs might make a difference. When selecting chickens, remember that you don't need roosters for egg laying. Roosters are loud, can be obnoxious, and are illegal to keep in many jurisdictions. You'll do better with three or four hens that can live together peacefully and lay eggs.

Chickens need basic shelter and enough space to roam a little. Their shelter need not be a formal chicken coop or animal hutch, but could be any appropriate small structure that you can either construct or commandeer. For example, an old toolshed or doghouse might work, or you could build your own shelter from some wooden crates or salvaged lumber. A small 2' W x 4' L x 2' H coop could be space enough for a pair of smaller chickens. An 8' x 12' coop can accommodate up to 30 regular-sized chickens, but you should avoid overcrowding or else you will risk stress, disease, and unproductive hatching.[71] Using chicken wire and a frame, you can either build in a small yard or run outside the main structure, or let them roam free when they come outside. Cover the bottom of the chicken house with some sand and a layer of bedding material (known as "litter"), which could be 3 to 4 inches of straw or untreated wood chips, or more in colder weather.[72] The sustainable living magazine *Mother Earth News* recently ran an article with plans for building your own small, portable 3' x 10' mini–chicken coop for about $100 worth of materials.[73] The article is accessible online in the *Mother Earth News* archives; just visit the website www.motherearthnews.com and type the words "Portable Chicken Coop" into the search box at the top; this article should come up first. This magazine, by the way, is geared mostly toward rural homesteaders and country-based gardeners, but every issue is so jam-packed with information that I frequently learn something new that I can apply in the city. To me, this is easily worth the very small subscription cost, which is further subsidized by some interesting advertisements. For other chicken coop building plans, try an Internet search or seek out a book (there are several in print) that covers some different coop designs.

You also can purchase chicken coops ready-made from pet stores and feed stores. The price varies with size, materials, and complexity. My Pet Chicken (www.mypetchicken.com) sells a small A-frame hutch for $99 and a deluxe 6-chicken pen and coop for $1,250. Shop the Coop (www.shopthecoop.com) sells coop heaters and Amish handcrafted nesting boxes, which can be added to your chicken house if needed. Critter Cages (www.critter-cages.com) and the McMurray Hatchery (www.mcmurrayhatchery.com) have plywood chicken coops, yards, and hutches as well as individual nesting boxes. Ware Manufacturing makes a number of coops that are sold by pet stores and online retailers; you can view their products and find a local retailer by visiting www.waremfginc.com. You also may want to check the eBay auction site for some additional options.

Whatever structure you use for a chicken house should provide some protection from the elements and from extreme temperatures. In mild climates, the building alone should shield them from any wind and rain, but in colder winter areas, you may need to both insulate and heat the structure.[74] Optimum temperature range for egg laying is between about 55 and 85 degrees F .[75] There are many types of acceptable structures for this, and some are handmade. During the winter in a cold climate, if you do not want to heat or insulate, then you could consider bringing this coop into a garage or greenhouse for protection, at least during the night. Since egg laying is a function of day length, you can encourage egg laying in colder weather by installing a regular incandescent lightbulb and leaving it on.

Inside the chicken house, you also should place some nesting spots and places for chickens to roost (sit up off the ground). The roosts can be anywhere they can climb up and sit, such as a shelf or ladder made of small dowels. The nesting areas, which encourage egg laying, should be fairly tight wooden boxes measuring about 14 inches on each side and about 12 inches deep.[76] An unused shoe rack with individual-sized boxes or a few old tool drawers may do the trick, but you could easily make some boxes yourself out of any available wood.

It's good to protect against other dangers as well. Wild predators are not the problem in the city that they are in the country, but even dogs and cats can do great damage to an unprotected flock. Also, though I live in an urban area, we occasionally see owls, crows, raccoons, and opossums as well as plenty of squirrels. These animals can either steal eggs or harm the chickens themselves if both are not protected, particularly at night. Chicken wire or poultry wire, available at hardware stores, has a small enough mesh that it should keep out any predators. The chicken house, and perhaps the entire coop, should be surrounded by chicken wire. Ideally, you should make a "floor" of chicken wire as well to seal in the coop, which still allows the chickens to peck at the ground below if you have their pen or a lawn or bare earth. With no chicken wire base, you need to be extra careful to weight down the sides with a wooden or metal frame, so that no predator can push up the wire or dig beneath it to make an entry hole. Make one mistake and you're bound to lose some chickens, and any survivors may be too stressed out to lay eggs for a while.

Once you have a space for your birds, you will need to decide what kind to get. Chickens available for purchase normally are bred for their suitability for eggs, for meat, or for both purposes. Bantam chickens are smaller-sized miniatures that are popular in many home yards, and other types are larger or medium-sized birds. The Leghorn breed is one of the most prolific egg layers, and they produce most commercial white-shelled eggs in North America. Other good egg layers include Ancona and Minorca chickens, both European breeds.[77] So-called dual-purpose chickens—American breeds such as Plymouth Rock, Rhode Island Red, and New Hampshire—do not lay eggs as quickly as Leghorns, but are still quite suitable for egg laying.[78] Also, consider that some breeds may be more cold tolerant than others or a better fit for your climate in general.

Buying commercial chicken feed is the easiest way to ensure your chickens get balanced food, and it's a good way to start out, but you can reduce costs over time by allowing them to supplement their diet through foraging. Chickens enjoy eating your fruit and vegetable scraps as long as you avoid giving them anything strong-tasting (for example, onions or garlic), which can affect the flavor of eggs.[79] Bread scraps and grass clippings are also good chicken food. But do not feed them any more than what they can eat in 10 to 20 minutes, or else their diets may become imbalanced.[80] You also can feed them whole grains to cut down on costs, but limit this to ½ pound per ten chickens to maintain balance. Scattering these grains on the ground encourages them to scratch the litter for their food, which will aerate it and keep it in better condition.[81] You can purchase feeders and waterers fairly cheaply online or from pet or feed stores. Finally, make sure you change the litter in the coop frequently (the bedding and manure, when aged, make great compost), gather eggs once or twice per day, and maintain the chickens' living quarters in a sanitary condition, which often means limiting outside moisture and keeping things dry.[82]

For further reading, I recommend *Barnyard in Your Backyard* and *Storey's Guide to Raising Chickens*, both by Gail Damerow. The first of these books might even encourage you to look beyond chickens to ducks for eggs, goats for milk and cheese, and other farm critters that could find a home in a larger urban backyard. Both books are highly accessible and informative guides.

HONEYBEES

I am not a beekeeper. I have known beekeepers. I have watched them look after their bees and have been fortunate that some have shared their knowledge and honey with me. Each time I have tasted raw, local honey, I have wished that I had my own colony of bees. But I guess everything takes time and we need to pick our paths. For now I have my hands full with many of the other pursuits mentioned in this book, not to mention a family and a full-time professional life. But I do hope to try raising my own bees someday, and I hope you will consider it also.

Since I am not an expert, my information comes from books and from others who have raised bees and told me about it. And there are a number of reasons that we should all consider raising bees, which reportedly take less work than other animals you could keep. They also do the world a lot of good by pollinating our plants and trees. And of course they produce delicious honey, which is a valued commodity that you can eat, share, and sell if need be.

Your first step in considering whether to raise bees, as with chickens, should be to examine local ordinances and make sure there are no restrictions on keeping bees in your county, city, neighborhood, or building. Bees can be loud and they can sting, so you'll also need to make sure that no one in your family, nor the immediate neighborhood, has allergies to bee stings.[83] Once again, offering to share some honey the first year with neighbors might mitigate adverse reactions to the idea of your keeping bees.

Bees have a place in the city. Wherever there are flowering plants and trees, we need bees to pollinate them, and the urban green roof movement is accelerating this demand. Chicago, which has been a leader in retrofitting many downtown buildings with green roofs, has a City Hall building with both a green roof and an apiary of bees on top.[84] The roofs of the famous old opera building in Paris and posh Fortnum & Mason in London's busy Piccadilly Square are two more examples of famous urban buildings that play host to colonies of bees.[85] In addition to their pollination services, bees provide honey as a nice byproduct, and this is the reason many become beekeepers.

A beehive can fit well in many urban spaces, yielding delicious honey as well as beeswax. ©iStockphoto.com/martb

If you have an outside area that is bordered by a hedge or fence, then this could be a perfect place for a hive, shielding the bees from neighbors' view. In addition, such a barrier can force bees to fly higher on take-off, minimizing the dangers of human interaction.[86] Beehives do not need to be in full sunlight, and even in cold temperatures, bees work to seal off the hive from wind and they cluster in the center of the structure where their combined body heat can keep the colony going through a cold winter. According to *Backyard Beekeeper* author Kim Flottum, keeping bees takes more work over the course of a season than keeping a cat, but less work than keeping a dog.[87] That may be an underestimation with the more recent disease problems that have resulted in a honeybee die-off in many regions, but with adequate research and preparation, you can become a successful urban beekeeper even on a small scale.

Keeping bees is a commitment, just like keeping pets. Before taking on such a responsibility, you would be wise to talk to some local beekeepers in your area and perhaps see if you can spend a day with one of them and his/her hives. There are a number of state and local associations across the United States and around the world. The San Francisco Beekeepers Association (www.sfbee.org) offers an introductory beekeeping class for both members and nonmembers; for those who do not have space for their own hives, the association also can host your hive for a small fee. The Vermont Beekeepers Association (www.vtbeekeepers.org) also provides workshops for novices, as well as a mentoring program with experienced beekeepers. A former president, Ross Conrad, wrote the book *Natural Beekeeping: Organic Approaches to Modern Apiculture.*[88] The Texas Beekeepers' Association (www.texas beekeepers.org) has an extensive network of local affiliates that hold regular meetings and provide support to novices. The Toronto District Beekeepers Association (www.torontobeekeepers.org) offers prospective beekeepers an opportunity to meet with experienced beekeepers and discuss the craft. (They also hold a honey-tasting competition.) Try searching on the Internet or checking with your local Cooperative Extension agent to see if there is an active beekeeping club in your area that could give you some advice on starting up.

Beginning beekeeping kits, which generally include two hives with eight frames as well as the basic equipment you need to get started, cost in the neighborhood of $215 at Betterbee (www.betterbee.com). Dadant Beekeeping (www.dadant.com/catalog) and Golden Bee (www.golden-bee.com) sell basic kits beginning around $150. If you decide to start with a kit, make sure that it is made of durable materials and that it can accommodate expansion with more frames and hives in the future. And before buying anything, I would advise approaching your local association or a neighborhood beekeeper for some advice on how to get started.

Another reason to start local is that you will, at some point, need some bees. And while you can mail order them, bees do not transport all that well. They can die or get stressed in transit, plus you may not know whether a particular variety is well suited to your region. Getting locally proven and healthy bees from someone in your area, if at all possible, is the way to go. If these are not available or if you need to re-queen, then order from a reputable mail-order source; your local beekeeping group should be able to recommend some. And before getting any bees, it is instructive to take a class or read a beginners' beekeeping guide such as one of the books mentioned above, that can teach you about the different types of available honeybees and their attributes, advantages, and disadvantages. These include their tendency to swarm or defend the hive as well as their winter cold-hardiness and their proneness or resistance to certain diseases.

Speaking of diseases, the onset of colony collapse disorder (CCD) in many regions of Europe and North America has deservedly received some media attention in the last few years. CCD is a term coined to describe the sudden disappearance of worker bees from a colony, which causes it to collapse suddenly. For reasons that are not entirely understood, more than two-thirds of the managed bee population in North America has died off in the course of the last few seasons following similar reports in Europe. This follows a dramatic decline in our wild honeybee population, which has been a trend for some time. Since at least 30 percent of our world's fruit and vegetable crops need bee pollination, CCD is an extremely serious issue for humans as well as a cautionary flag for would-be beekeepers. Scientists do not fully understand whether CCD has resulted from pathogens, tracheal or varroa mites, pesticide use, climate change, or other factors. Since bees pick up whatever is out there in our environment, even the small-scale hobby-ist beekeeper needs to be proactively prepared to combat mite infesta-tions and disease problems. You owe it to yourself, as well as your future colony of bees, to research your responsibilities fully before taking them on. That being said, there is so much to be gained from beekeeping, and your bees provide such a service to the world around you, that I hope you do strongly consider this noble pursuit.

eleven

MAKING COMPOST AND PARTNERING WITH WORMS

Plants grow well in soil that has healthy amounts of organic matter mixed in. This is very important for container gardeners, since the soil in containers needs to hold moisture, drain well, and be loose enough to allow oxygen to reach the roots. Compost is the ultimate organic matter, because it represents living plant tissue that has been decomposed through the action of microbes, earthworms, and other organisms. Finished compost is a stable soil that still teems with beneficial organisms, and these can add vitality and immunity, as well as nutrition, to your plants.

Compost can be made from any plant matter, including lawn clippings, tree leaves, food scraps, newspaper, and/or manure from animals that have eaten plants (such as cows, horses, sheep, rabbits, and worms). Whether you are gardening with containers or in the ground, your soil will benefit from added compost. Most good soil mixes incorporate some composted matter, and organic fertilizers usually contain small amounts of composted manure or seed meal, so chances are that you are already getting some of the benefits of compost for your plants.

Over time, you will need to add more. If you are gardening in the ground and using soil that contains compost or organic matter, then your soil will settle over time, and you will notice the soil level dropping in your growing beds. This is largely due to the work of earthworms and other soil-based organisms, which transport organic matter deeper into the soil as they continue to transform and improve it. Each growing season, you will need to add more soil, and you simply cannot do better than heaping more compost on top.

Even if you are container gardening, where the number of earthworms is few to none, you will lose some of your dirt each time you pull out plants at the end of a growing season. Your top few inches of soil will be scraped off at the end of each season and will need to be refreshed with new fertilizer. So a container garden also requires a few extra inches of soil on a regular basis. Compost is a great addition to your container soil and makes a wonderful top mulch that retains moisture and conserves heat for the plants' roots.

So if compost is such great stuff, where can you get some? You can buy bags of something called compost in garden stores, but be careful to read the ingredients list. If the first ingredient is forest waste, then check to see whether it is just shredded wood bark (which takes many years to really decompose, and should not be the first ingredient in your soil) or is dark, finely composted humus from dead leaves (which is very good stuff). You will need to look at the soil itself to determine this; a quick look should tell you whether it is dark and fine-grained or just shreds of bark. Further down the ingredients list may appear poultry manure, bat guano, kelp meal, or seed meal, all of which boost the nutrient levels considerably, but do not change the fact that shredded bark makes a better pathway mulch than growing medium. Any bagged compost that is based on yard waste, leaf mould, or a diversity of sources should be better. If municipal waste is an ingredient, make sure this does not come from human sewage solids; this stuff is well treated and clean, but it contains higher levels of heavy metals than you want in your food-growing soil.

Manure is another form of compost that is readily available for sale in different forms; you can sometimes get bagged manure from garden stores or pick up as much as you can carry from a dairy or horse stable. Animals have done some of the composting for us, though fresh manure must be further composted before using. (Look for "composted" or "aged" manure.) For ground-based urban gardens, manure is truly black gold, as it fertilizes your plants while encouraging earthworms and friendly soil-based organisms that will supercharge your soil. In container gardening, most manure is too hot to use as organic matter; it makes a better top-spread fertilizer. The exception to this is dairy manure or any stuff that comes with a lot of hay or bedding material; this may limit its potency and make it benign enough to mix into your container soil. Make sure that any manure you use is fully composted before adding it to your soil, as the hot-composting process will kill any pathogens.

The following chart shows the major nutrient (N-P-K) composition of common livestock manures; bear in mind that these figures really depend on the diet these animals are fed and other variables, but this is a good place to start.

MAJOR NUTRIENT COMPOSITION OF COMMON MANURES

	Percent composition		
Fertilizer	**N**	**P_2O_5**	**K_2O**
Cow manure	0.5-2.0	0.2-0.9	0.5-1.5
Horse manure	0.5-2.5	0.3-2.5	0.5-3.0
Sheep manure	1.0-4.0	1.0-2.5	1.0-3.0
Rabbit manure, dry	2.3-3.0	1.4-2.0	0.6-1.0
Poultry manure	1.1-6.0	0.5-4.0	0.5-3.0
Hog manure	0.3-0.5	0.2-0.4	0.4-0.5

Sources: Colorado State University Extension[89] and the Dirt Doctor[90]

But let me be clear: You do not need to use manure at all, in any form, in your urban garden. If you prefer not to use it or are concerned about odors or hygiene, other types of compost and fertilizer certainly can grow you a magnificent food garden. If you can't buy good compost, then you can always make it yourself, or get some worms to do it for you. First, here is some information on making your own compost; we will follow this with a guide to partnering with worms, who can do the dirty work for you!

MAKING COMPOST

You can make your own compost using a traditional compost pile or with a bin or tumbler. Most apartment and condo dwellers have little or no ground space, which probably means you will not be able to start a compost pile. Imagine a balcony in a high-rise apartment building in New York City, hanging a hundred feet above a busy street, covered with a fetid, dripping mass of kitchen waste. This is why compost tumblers and worm bins were invented, and both of them allow you to recycle your solid waste products in a clean, tidy, and nearly odor-free manner. We'll cover these contraptions in a bit.

Composting is a pretty amazing process. It recycles nearly any living matter back into a stable elemental soil that can feed the next generation of plants. In addition to yielding a rich growing soil and recycling our food and yard waste, the process itself has far-reaching benefits for cleaning up our world. According to the U.S. Environmental Protection Agency, "the composting process has been shown to absorb odors and treat semivolatile and volatile organic compounds (VOCs), including heating fuels, polyaromatic hydrocarbons (PAHs), and explosives. It has also been shown to bind heavy metals and prevent them from migrating to water resources or being absorbed by plants. The compost process degrades and, in some cases, completely eliminates wood preservatives, pesticides, and both chlorinated and nonchlorinated hydrocarbons in contaminated soils."[91] Although I do not advocate adding chemicals to your compost pile, this just shows how amazing these composting organisms are, and how composting can play an important role in cleaning up and restoring our world. You can play your own small part, and save yourself money on buying bagged material, by beginning your own small composting system at home.

STARTING A TRADITIONAL COMPOST PILE

If you have enough space to start a compost pile in your yard, make sure your local city and county ordinances permit it. Some of them have restrictions because open piles can attract rodents and create odors. Assuming that your area allows open-air composting, consider whether you can fit three piles in your yard: one for new compost, one for aging compost, and one for the finished stuff that goes back on your plants. If you just have room for one, that is fine, but in order for your pile to fully break down, you will need to stop adding new material at some point and let it decompose.

Some compost piles are hot, while others never get very warm, and this is a function of the biological activity in the pile while the organisms do their thing. Getting your pile to heat up naturally depends on a long list of factors, including pile size, materials, layering, moisture, external heat, and other variables. But even if it does not heat up much, sooner or later the stuff will break down and you'll have some good dirt to use on your plants. Cold compost is perfectly acceptable stuff; it just takes a bit longer to make.[92] Some gardening purists hold that the nutritional content of hot-cooked compost is far superior, but if you are using it as more of a soil amendment than a fertilizer, then this should not matter much. If you want to follow the pure wisdom, then the minimum size for a hot pile is about 4'x 4', which will allow enough internal space to create the proper conditions for this biological activity to take place.[93] In lieu of this, any untidy heap will break down at its own pace.

What should you put in your compost pile? Will it stink? Do you have to turn it regularly? The answers are: anything organic, a bit, and not really. Dead leaves, lawn clippings, food scraps (except meat or fat), newspaper, cardboard, and manure are all organic matter and will break down in your compost pile. Ideally, you want to add a diversity of ingredients. The pile will break down faster if you add both "browns" (dry ingredients such as dead leaves, newspaper, and cardboard) and "greens" (wet stuff such as food scraps, lawn clippings, and fresh manure). "Greens" contain plenty of nitrogen while "browns" have more carbon, and your pile needs both. Conventional wisdom holds that the proper ratio is 2 parts "browns" to 1 part "greens," but you can vary this ratio somewhat. Just remember that a pile of 100 percent leaves takes a lot longer to break down, and 100 percent food scraps may turn into a very wet and slimy mess long before it breaks down.[94] Also, the more diverse sources of waste you add, the better its nutritional output will be for your soil.

Your new pile will stink a bit at first, but if you have never composted before, then you will be pleasantly surprised. It's not as smelly as you would think. In its early stages, you can cover the compost pile with burlap, a tarp, or a layer of "brown" ingredients such as leaves or cardboard, which will help seal in the moisture and limit any odors. As the compost ages, it begins to smell more earthy, a fragrance that some actually enjoy. Your compost is finished when you can no longer recognize the individual materials that went into it.

Aerating the pile is optional, but it may speed up the process by delivering oxygen where it's needed. Use a pitchfork to turn the pile and make sure that both air and moisture are reaching each part. You can do this weekly or less often. And, if you do not want to turn the pile, then it will aerate naturally with time as the layers break down and settle.[95]

NATURAL LAYERING, WITH AND WITHOUT A BIN

Layering is the natural order of decomposition. In nature, when rotten fruit falls, then a tree loses its leaves, and maybe an animal walks by and fertilizes the spot, no one comes by with a pitchfork to turn and aerate these materials. They decompose because the various organisms that feed on these sources can naturally break them down from their layers, and over time they will settle into a unified mass of soil. In the 1970s and '80s, permaculture advocates in Australia and elsewhere popularized a method of organic gardening known as "no-dig" gardening, which was a technique that Japanese gardener Masanobu Fukuoka had practiced in an extreme form for many years.[96] [97] Their concept was basically to let things layer naturally and to refrain from tilling the soil. Patricia Lanza, in her classic book *Lasagna Gardening*, took this a step further by suggesting that gardeners build their compost layers directly on top of the garden soil, popularizing the concept of "sheet composting."[98] The terms "sheet mulching" and "interbay mulching" also refer to variations on this same concept. This natural (though gardener-assisted) organic layering encourages earthworms and soil organisms to play their part, and it results in some of the finest soil you can imagine.

If you are gardening directly in the ground and want to try this layering for yourself, then spread alternating layers of "browns" and "greens" right onto your soil. If you have access to a little manure, seed meal, cornmeal, coffee grounds, seaweed, or any other rich source of nutrients, throw it in and make a layer of it. Cover the last layer with leaves, straw, cardboard, or soil, and let nature take its course. As the layers decompose, the level will drop, and you can continue adding layers to the top as you prefer. In a few months to a year, your soil will be teeming with earthworms, and this will be the finest growing soil on the planet. But it does take a little time.

No one (aside from soil scientists) really knows why or can explain how this layered decomposition works better than mixing everything

A compost bin can fit almost anywhere, either over garden soil or on a patio. ©iStockphoto.com/davidf

together, but it does work, probably because the materials are layered in nature. On a smaller scale, you can practice this same concept in a compost bin (the type that does not get turned). Buy a plastic one or build your own square or rectangular bin from wood, but it must have an open base or one that opens. Add layers of compost into your bin, don't turn it, and then "harvest" your finished compost from the bottom. If the base of the bin is open and directly in the soil, then simply move the bin, spread your compost, and start the layered pile again elsewhere. A list of several commercial sources for bins appears in the next section.

BUILDING A BED ON THE PATIO

We have a patio area covered with textured concrete. Part of it has a shady section away from the house, which mostly gets reflected light off a stucco wall. The light is enough to grow leafy greens and root vegetables in the containers I have placed there. I also have used it as a home for my compost tumbler, which is braced above the ground with a steel frame and spins on a horizontal axle. Because of the shade and location, no one else in the family seemed too interested in using that space, so I did not get any objections about the compost tumbler. Until recently, I had not thought of using this space for anything else.

Some time ago, I became interested in sheet mulching, which I started to practice in the small strip of ground soil we have access to on the other side of our home. This is the sunny side, where we have a couple of raised-bed planters along a sidewalk, each of which is open to the ground below. To improve the soil in these planters, which was heavy clay under about three inches of good topsoil, I dug down and removed about 12 inches of clay, replacing it with progressive layers of compost "browns" and "greens." As the pile decomposed and the level dropped, I covered it with a few more layers and then with the original topsoil. Worms came up to eat the decomposing matter, loosening the clay beneath and enriching the soil. In a few months, with the heat of the sun, I ended up with some of the richest gardening soil I could imagine.

Then recently, I was thumbing through a fun little book called

Composting: An Easy Household Guide by Nicky Scott.[99] I noticed the words, "Composting . . . will work on concrete, provided there is good drainage." I read on and he elaborated, "Worms will find their way across tarmac and concrete to colonize your heap." He suggested using a good bedding material like moist cardboard, which worms like. I was intrigued, but I still couldn't afford to start a stinky compost pile on my patio. But, later that evening, suddenly everything clicked in my brain: I could build a sheet-mulched growing bed in that half-shady corner of my patio; no one would even know it was full of compost, and I would be able to grow all the greens I wanted over there once it was finished.

The next morning, which happened to be a Saturday, I made my excuses to the family for an hour or two, and dashed outside. I moved my compost tumbler a few feet, clearing some space, and covered the patio drain with a few handfuls of stones so that it would not get plugged up with dirt. I rummaged through the recycling bin, finding two flattened cardboard boxes and some newspaper. Then I realized that I should really start with some worms, since this would speed up the process greatly. A few days before, I had been planting a plum tree in a nearby yard and had carted over a little extra topsoil that came with a little grass and worms. So I started by covering my concrete patio floor with some of this real dirt, including the worms and grass. This I covered with the cardboard and paper. On top of the cardboard, I added a layer of alfalfa hay that I had been using as a high-protein mulch. (Alfalfa hay is a "green" because it has lots of nitrogen.) I covered this with some more "browns": newspaper, ripped-up brown paper shopping bags, and a few leaves I had taken from the main sidewalk. I wetted down the whole pile so it wouldn't fall over. Food scraps went on top, including some apple cores, banana skins, potato and kiwi peelings, broccoli trimmings, old bread, used coffee grounds, and a sprinkling of cornmeal. Before anyone could see this part, I covered it with a thick layer of peat that I had purchased. (One could also use free "brown" sources like hay, cardboard, or leaves on top, but I had not collected enough at this point.) I then threw some potting soil on top and piled it around the sides for appearances. And I wet this down once as well. The pile was about 12 inches high, as high as I could manage without it falling over, and it looked for all the world like a big bed of potting soil.

Now, a couple of months later, my sheet-mulch/compost pile still looks like a bed of soil and is decomposing quickly, yet thanks to the "brown" layer of peat and soil on top, there are no odors and I have not seen any pests. (Coffee grounds also help to deodorize things.) I have continued adding layers: some ripped-up newspaper, food scraps, and another layer of potting soil. I cannot yet report on the results because the pile is still decomposing, but I will say this: I cheated and plunged a shovel into the new bed to see how the soil looked. The layers were decomposing very quickly and I could see earthworms everywhere, far more than I had introduced at the beginning. This soil is going to be way better than any potting soil. If I wanted to, I could probably plant into it right now, but I will wait a little longer to do so. My reason for waiting is that the height keeps dropping with decomposition; I will need to keep adding layers and building it up a little higher. What begins as 12 inches decomposes to much less than that, and to make a bed of soil that is deep enough for planting, I will need to add to the pile a few more times. Then I may decide to frame it with a few cinderblocks or pieces of wood, just so that I can build it higher without it spilling over. The soil then will be deep enough for me to grow some good veggies over there: Even squash or potatoes may have just enough light!

A patio-based sheet-mulch bed is a radical step; it is not as tidy as a container, and building it does take some work. But you can build one completely with waste materials and keep it reasonably tidy looking as well. When the reward is a lifetime of good soil for healthy planting, I consider the time and trouble of building this bed to be a very worthwhile investment. Because of the important role that earthworms and soil microbes play, this process would be more difficult to re-create inside a container. Nevertheless, this bed is just one of my growing areas; as a city dweller with limited space, I will continue to use containers to grow many of my staple vegetables. Making compost or worm castings elsewhere and then mixing these into container soil will produce excellent results as well.

Urban compost bins are attractive, hygienic, and come in many styles. ©iStockphoto.com/Ms_Ash

URBAN TUMBLING

No, it's not the latest exercise craze. A compost tumbler is a plastic bin or other holding container that stores your compost, allows you to turn it easily for aeration, and keeps the temperature warm enough so the compost can finish more quickly than it would in the outside air. Some of these are mounted on frames to allow turning, and there are a variety of other creative product designs that are said to promote internal solar heat, aeration, and ease of use. Although urban-sized tumblers or self-contained bins may not make the most nutritious compost (or even cook it any faster than a pile would), they have tremendous advantages for urban dwellers in that they are tight, clean methods of keeping your compost away from the noses of neighbors and the reach of rodents.[100] A small tumbler or bin can fit easily in a patio or on a porch, making urban composting a reality. They also are encouraged, rather than restricted, by many local governments; see whether your city or county government provides bins at a discounted rate (mine does, but only for bins and not tumblers). Some Internet mail-order sources include www.composters.com, www.gardeners .com, www.4seasongreenhouse.com, and www.ebay.com. Also see the sources listed for worm bins below.

PARTNERING WITH WORMS

Any book about urban food production would be incomplete without mentioning worms. Although I do not advocate eating worms as food, there are two reasons an urban gardener should consider raising them. First, worms can generate very healthful fertilizer for your plants that is known to make them stronger and more pest-resistant. Second, worms are probably the simplest pets you can ever keep: A worm bin takes up just one or two square feet of floor space on a balcony or garage floor, and its residents ask for nothing more than your food scraps. A worm bin is the ultimate urban recycling system for food scraps, since their castings provide excellent nutrition for plants using the waste you would otherwise throw away. And if you decide to grow worms for bait sale, then this could be an extra source of cash in some regions. A few backyard gardeners have even worked to create a mostly closed system whereby they raise fish for food, use the worms to feed the fish, use their food scraps to feed the worms, and use the worm and fish excrement to grow the vegetables.[101] However, it cannot be a completely closed system as long as human sewage is flushed down the toilet, because this represents a huge net loss of nutrients we have taken from the soil. Short of composting your own *humanure* (a prospect that is repulsive to most people and probably impossible in a city), you always will need outside sources of nutrients added into the system.[102] In a closed system based on fish farming, you also would need a way to convert the ammonia waste from fish into nitrogen that plants can use, which requires an extra composting step with particular bacteria. And all of this would take much more space than most of us have in the city, which is why we now return to our topic of small-scale worm composting!

In order to keep worms, you need a home for them. It should be located in a place with moderate temperatures, such as a garage or laundry room. (Remember, worms do not need sunlight.) Alternately, you could keep them on a porch or balcony if temperatures are not too extreme. Worm bins (sometimes called worm composters or vermicomposters) can be purchased from several Internet suppliers. Before buying at retail prices, however, check with your local city and county governments to see whether they encourage composting. In San Mateo County, California, for example, local residents can purchase compost bins and worm bins from the county itself at about half the regular cost. The city of Seattle also subsidizes composter and worm bin purchases from certain suppliers. Vancouver, British Columbia, provides many incentives and even maintains a hotline for residents to call with composting questions.[103] If you need to buy from a supplier, then your local garden center may have a model, but you should check the Internet for many more possibilities and prices. Some suppliers with good selections of worm composters are Worms.com (www.worms.com or 1-800-compost), Composters.com (www.composters.com), All Things Organic (www.allthingsorganic .com), and Abundant Earth (www.abundantearth.com).

You will notice right away that worm bins and composters tend to be expensive. Besides checking to see if your local government subsidizes

Worms can help to compost kitchen scraps, yielding nutritious fertilizer for your plants. ©iStockphoto.com/PhillDanze

them, I have two other possible suggestions for reducing your expenses here. First, see if you can get a secondhand worm bin. Some people buy one thinking it's a great idea, and they tire of it after six months or a year. By checking eBay and local classified ads, as well as garage sales and flea markets, you may be able to find a worm bin that is almost new and walk away with it for a few dollars. The second suggestion is to build your own, and it's not that difficult. We will discuss some simple building plans below, but first, here are some tips on what to look for when buying a worm bin.

There are several key features to consider in a worm bin. The first is size and shape: Does it fit in your available space? Most worm bins are pretty small, but make sure it fits. I do not recommend keeping worm bins indoors except in a garage or basement, since they will give off a mild odor and may attract a few fruit flies. Second, the best bins have multiple levels or trays, which allow for easy feeding and collection of worm castings. The idea is that you put your food scraps in one tray and the worms eat them. Once they are finished with that one, they migrate to the next tray of food through holes in the bottom, and the first tray can be removed so you can empty the worm castings. You then restack the emptied tray and begin the cycle again. This is much easier than trying to take worm castings out of a bin full of worms, so look for bins that have at least two levels or trays. Third, there is the small problem (and opportunity) of the bottom getting wet. The drippings from worm compost are full of nutrients, and can be collected and diluted to use as a compost tea fertilizer or foliar feed for plants. A good worm bin will have a tray to catch any drippings, and a great worm bin will have a catchment container or a spout from which you can drain off the compost tea. Finally, consider that wet wood can rot over time, so bins made of plastic last longer.

How can you make your own worm bin? Start with a plastic bin that fits your space. As with self-watering planter boxes, you can make your own worm bin out of a Rubbermaid or Sterilite container or storage box, which normally costs less than $5 at your local hardware store or home center. Get the right size to fit your space. Better yet, buy two identical plastic bins with lids so that you can create two levels for the wigglers and make your job easier. A single-level worm bin would simply be a plastic container with a cover on and holes drilled in the sides and the bottom. The side holes are for air circulation and the bottom holes are primarily for drainage. You should also have a tray (perhaps an extra lid?) beneath the bin to catch any drippings. To make a two-level worm bin with two plastic containers, follow these directions. You will need the two plastic bins with lids, a third lid or catchment tray about the same size, a drill with a ¼ inch bit, and four small blocks of wood or stones to serve as feet for the bins to rest on. (You could also construct a simple stand by cutting a wooden stake into pieces.)

1. Turn one bin upside down. Take one of the lids, and place it over the bottom of the upturned bin so that you can drill through both surfaces at once. The lid also should be upside down. Using a drill with a ¼ inch bit, drill 20 to 30 small holes through the lid and bin bottom at the same time. These should be evenly spaced, since the worms will

be crawling through when they migrate through the bins. Next, turn over the second bin. Using the holey lid as a template, drill the bottom of the second bin with holes.

2. On the sides of each bin, drill a few ventilation holes (about 10 per bin should be enough). Make sure that some of the holes are near the top of the sides, since this will allow air to circulate above the worms' food and bedding.

3. You will start the worms in the bin with the holey lid and stack the second bin on top. The bottom bin should always be propped up with blocks or a stand to allow air circulation underneath. When the bottom bin starts to get full of castings and depleted of food, you will fill it once more with food or wet newspaper up to the top. Then you will stop adding food to the bottom bin and begin adding it to the top bin instead. In about one month, nearly all of the worms will have migrated through to their new home in the top bin, and you can safely take out the bottom bin to harvest the castings. Then you will swap lids and stack the newly emptied bin on top, completing the cycle.

4. An alternative, if you need to save space, is to use only one bin for the worms until it's time to change bins. In this scenario, you would use the solid lid to cover the worm bin, and only when it is time to make the transition would you replace this with the holey lid, stack the second, empty bin on top, and induce the worms to move. If the bin is kept outdoors in a shady spot, you could even cover it with a small planter box.

A worm bin is not complete without two additional ingredients: bedding material and worms. Shredded newspaper or cardboard makes good bedding material, but coco fiber coir or peat moss (with lime added to stabilize pH) are even better. Sprinkle in a few handfuls of garden soil, sand, or cornmeal to add some grit, and wet down the bedding until it is damp. You now can add the worms. Regular earthworms do not make the best composters, so you should obtain some composting worms. Redworms or red wigglers (*Eisenia fetida*) make the best composters and are the easiest worms to order. You often can get them from a local bait shop for a few dollars. Alternatively, you could dig into a local compost pile and collect the worms that you find, which is a bit riskier but costs nothing.[104] You also can order worms over the Internet; check the worm bin suppliers listed above or the eBay site for a number of options. Once you put the worms in, feed them slowly at first, and as they get acclimated and reproduce you can increase their food. If there is still extra food from the previous day, then reduce the input until they start to eat it all. In the worm composting bible *Worms Eat My Garbage*, author Mary Appelhof recommends a 2:1 ratio of worms to food per day, meaning that 1,000 worms (which is 2 pounds) can go through about 1 pound of food per day.[105] You can feed them any vegetable or food scraps except for citrus, onions, or garlic, which they dislike. Bread, cereals, coffee grounds, and tea leaves are good worm food also. Do not add any meat, dairy, or oils to the worm bin and avoid anything that can't be easily broken down, such as fruit pits or very woody stems. Make sure that the contents of the bin do not dry out (the dampness of a wrung-out sponge is about right), and if you go on vacation for a week or so, just add a little extra food before you leave. To limit fruit flies, you can cover the food scraps with cardboard or paper. Adding plenty of coffee grounds helps control odors.

One variation on this closed system would be to make a hybrid compost layering bin/worm bin that is open to the ground below. You could use a wooden crate, a plastic bucket punched with holes, or any bottomless container. The idea would be to have your compost rest directly on the soil so that worms could crawl up into it. Or you could add composting worms yourself. The worms would then have a home that was somewhat warmer than the natural soil. If using native earthworms (who cannot survive in pure compost and are accustomed to lower soil temperatures), then I would add layers of soil between compost to recreate their natural living conditions. Redworms and red wigglers, in contrast, are composting worms that have been imported from warmer climates; they cannot survive in pure soil or in most North American winters, so I would consider moving them to an indoor or garage-based bin during colder weather. And be sure to keep it moist or damp; a worm's body is 75 to 90 percent water, and it needs a damp surface to breathe.[106] Also see the section above on building a sheet-mulched bed on your patio, which is really very similar to a large worm bin that becomes a rich planting bed over time.

I cannot conclude any discussion of worm composting without recommending an amazing little book called *The Earth Moved* by Amy Stewart. It is not a "how-to" book, but rather a reflection and synthesis of wisdom on the achievements of earthworms and their importance to human civilization. Did you know, for example, that Charles Darwin focused all his research in later years on earthworms and was the first scientist to suggest that worms tilled the first few inches of soil on a regular basis? Did you know that major agricultural civilizations of ancient times were located in areas that contain some of the richest earthworm populations in the world? Or that our friendly earthworm poses a (perhaps fatal) threat to some forest ecosystems in North America? This is a truly fascinating story that should be required reading for all gardeners, and it's told by a gifted author who makes it both compelling and fun to read.[107]

twelve

SURVIVAL DURING RESOURCE SHORTAGES

I am not a survivalist by any stretch of the imagination, but I include some basic information here on surviving resource shortages because I think that, even as our civilization will probably survive the tough times ahead, there will be periods of disruption in the flow of resources, during which we may not be able to count on outside help. With the challenges of a growing population and increasing demand for energy and water (as well as food), it is wise to consider how we would function if a major supply disruption were to occur.

WHAT TO EXPECT IN THE YEARS AHEAD

"We live in an era of converging crises," as one commentator has written.[108] In the coming years, humanity faces the compounding challenges of global climate change, peak oil, diminishing returns from our agriculture, and other resource (including water) shortages stemming from overpopulation.[109] These are no longer fringe issues or abstract policy concerns, but real problems that threaten our way of life. It is difficult to imagine comprehensive solutions appearing overnight from our policymakers and through our market economy, though I am hopeful that both public and private spheres will produce some solutions in the longer term.

As resources become scarcer in the short term, the burden shifts to you and me to prepare for the inevitable consequences. This does not mean that there will be no water, no energy, and no food in the future, but as there is greater competition for the supply of these commodities, they become more costly and occasionally hard to obtain. You and I need to prepare for a time very soon when: (a) the things we need will cost a lot more, and (b) there may be some disruptions in supply. In a way, this whole book is about preparing for higher-cost items, since it is about raising your own food, which will keep your costs down significantly. However, this particular chapter deals with some other survival (and comfort) concerns related to periods when you face a shortage of some key resource, such as electricity, heat, food, or water.

HOW SHOULD YOU PREPARE?

You need to prepare for supply disruptions. This could be either a natural disaster or a manmade one. With water, it could be a pipeline rupture or severe rationing during a prolonged drought. With oil, it could be a terrorist attack or the news one day that the world's largest oil field, Saudi Arabia's Ghawar, has peaked in its production capability and is beginning its inevitable decline (which would signal the peak in global production capability). Our supplies of energy, and water in some regions, are stretched thin these days, and there is very little spare capacity left to feed our growing consumption. Also, the aftermath of Hurricane Katrina on the Gulf Coast proved that the government may not be able to respond quickly and effectively in a large-scale natural disaster such as an earthquake, tornado, flood, fire, hurricane, windstorm, or tsunami. In 2006 alone, hundreds of thousands of people from Seattle to St. Louis went without power for many days at a time during extreme hot or cold weather.

Laugh if you will, but I am not at all convinced that we will have endless supplies of all the resources we need. If a major disruption in water or energy does occur for some reason, will you be prepared? Notice that I am talking mostly of short-term disruptions here; I believe there may be prolonged periods when we have less energy or water than we are accustomed to having, and perhaps times when we have none at all. In addition, resources will be much more expensive than they are now, so we may choose to ration them ourselves. But I am also optimistic that humankind can respond creatively and constructively to the problems we face, including climate change, peak oil, and population growth. We have tremendous challenges to surmount in embracing alternate energy sources and transforming our civilization and economic system to one that is more sustainable and harmonious with the planet we have been given. I believe that we will do so. Otherwise, if I were pessimistic and believed civilization was about to end, I would drop everything, max out all my credit cards, and outfit a bunker in the mountains with a century's worth of canned food and other supplies. If everyone did this, then civilization *would* end; I am more concerned, though, with getting over the inevitable bumps in the road ahead.

Although I would love to live completely "off the grid" with solar and wind energy plus my own well water, it is not possible to live self-sufficiently in the city. Most readers probably do not have their own renewable energy supplies, so you are likely in the same boat as I am. How can you plan, on a smaller, urban scale, in case a resource supply disruption occurs?

SMALL-SCALE "OFF THE GRID" ENERGY SOLUTIONS

How would your family survive if you had no electricity to run lighting, heating, cooling, cooking, laundry, computers, and other household appliances? In northern climates, a cold winter without heat may be a survival issue, and it is at least a comfort issue for everyone else. If you had no heat for cooking, could your family survive on cold food every night? Do you have that many cans of beans? Could you read at night by candlelight? Do your own laundry by hand? There are a lot of things we take for granted in good times.

Where winters are freezing cold, many people own generators. A good generator is a worthy investment, but it runs on gas or other fuel, which may be impossible to get during tough times. Also, generators cannot be run indoors unless you want to poison your family's air. The good news is that there are a few alternate sources of small-scale power available. The bad news is that none of them are very powerful, so you will have to conserve energy and buy some backup equipment that can run on lower power. You probably have at least one source of backup power for your home already, and that is your car battery. In a pinch, any of the backup system components I describe here can be run with no more than your car battery. I would recommend that you get a second 12-volt battery for backup power that is more accessible when you need it, and that way your car battery can serve as a "backup backup." Consider purchasing a backup power pack such as some of the models made by Xantrex, Black & Decker, Schumacher, or Sentinel. With the Xantrex XPower packs, for example, you get a sealed, long-lasting 12-volt battery with both a DC jack and AC inverter plug that can be charged from any AC or DC source, including a solar panel, micro-wind turbine, or hand-crank generator. Many of these power packs also include jumper cables, emergency lights, and tire pumps, which are a nice bonus.

Besides power storage, the most important consideration is generating enough power to recharge the batteries and run the bare essentials. I am guessing that you do not have a full solar or wind power system in your urban home. However, if you have plenty of sun and access to a rooftop, you may want to consider investing in a small-scale solar system that can recharge a 12- volt car battery in a few hours. I have a portable, fold-up solar panel set under the bed that can charge a car battery in about eight hours, which is pretty pathetic, but it's something. Better yet, I have embraced the revolution in hand-cranked energy. In addition to several wind-up flashlights, high-output lanterns, and radios, I have a step generator that creates electricity from human-driven friction. During a blackout, it's time for a workout, and 30 to 40 minutes of solidly pumping my feet can fully charge a 12-volt battery. This is a truly remarkable yet simple invention that is now widely available to the public. I do not know of any other way to generate this much power so quickly through small-scale renewable means. I hope that other inventors and manufacturers are hard at work on some similar items. Information on the generator is available at www.freeplayenergy .com/products.

HEATING YOUR HOME

The next consideration is heating. It should go without saying that you need good weatherproofing for your home and a couple of extra sweaters. A fireplace, wood stove, or other alternate fuel stove is wonderful if you have one. Beyond that, how can you heat your home with no electricity? The best strategy is to try to heat the people in the home, not the whole home itself. As many long-haul truckers and RV drivers know, there are heating blankets available that run on car batteries. Better yet, because heat rises, a 12-volt-heated mattress pad is the perfect way to warm your body for a long period using very few watts of energy. Two good sources of 12V heaters and mattress pads are www.realtruck.com and www.cozywinters.com. There are also several low-wattage heating panels on the market that can heat part of a room quite efficiently. One widely available example is the Cozy Legs Heat panel, available through many online retailers.

After a recent Pacific storm, my family and I went through a 48-hour period with no electricity during one of the coldest weeks of the year. Granted, this was Northern California cold and not New England cold, but it was still a challenge. Coping with outages like this has helped me learn some valuable lessons to apply in the future. I mention these lessons here because some readers may be as naive as I once was; others of you, no doubt, are already a lot wiser than I am. First, I learned that heated blankets and mattress pads (running on a backup battery) go a long way, but it is good to have nonelectrical heat sources ready as well. Fireplaces do not generate as much heat for the home as wood stoves; if you have the choice and the money, go with a wood stove and get one with a surface that can boil water and heat food. This may be one of the best investments you can make. Say what you want about burning wood, but it is a renewable fuel and can provide a heat and cooking source for less than electricity is beginning to cost these days. Burning wood or wood pellets in an efficient stove releases less carbon dioxide into the atmosphere than if that same log had decayed in the forest. Second, I learned that gas appliances (including stoves and water heaters) will work fine during a power outage so long as their starter mechanisms are not electrical. Gas stoves with an automatic lighter, for example, need to be lit with a match. Some water heaters and gas furnaces have a pilot light that runs on gas. Gas, of course, is a limited resource also, so we should all prepare for times when this also may be in short supply. Third, flashlights are essential in the dark, but you need a couple of good lanterns as well to provide light when there is no electricity. Make a visit to a camping store and buy a kerosene lantern as well as one or two of the LED lanterns that work on batteries or wind-up crank power. There are also solar-powered lights available; BOGO lights provide 4–5 hours of LED illumination after solar-charging for 8 hours (www.bogolight.com). Surplus stores or eBay are other possible sources of LED lanterns and flashlights.

PREPARING FOR DISRUPTIONS IN THE FOOD AND WATER SUPPLY

In the event of any major regional disaster, such as a hurricane, earth-quake, or terrorist attack, the Red Cross and disaster planning agencies normally recommend that people be prepared to survive for up to 72 hours without outside assistance, but this is really a bare minimum. It is good to have some bottled water and canned food available for such times. You can do even better by purchasing a disaster or emergency kit, which may include not only military-style food ration bars and shelf-stable water but also first-aid supplies, space blankets, flashlights, cleansing wipes, and other basic tools and materials. Camping stores carry these kits, and they also are available by mail order from several online retailers; try an online search for "disaster kit," "emergency supplies," or something similar. Warning: Get one soon; some of these kits sell out near the beginning of hurricane season and it then can take months for them to fill your order.

Consider, though, that the situation could be much worse than a 72-hour need. In the aftermath of Hurricane Katrina in 2005, it took the federal government five days to do a major airdrop of food and water to their own designated shelter site in New Orleans.[110] And even after food and water is brought to a shelter or staging site, such as a convention center or National Guard armory, it may take much longer for it to reach people in far-flung locations. The Katrina disaster occurred during a time of plenty in our country. In the near future, fuel for transportation may be scarce, rationed, or prohibitively priced, and the government may be stretched thinner than it has been in the past. Imagine if there were an oil embargo, prolonged drought with water rationing, and then a disaster such as a hurricane, earthquake, or terrorist attack that struck a wide geographic area. I am not advocating a full-scale survivalist bunker mentality here, but it is better to prepare than not to prepare. Be safe and plan ahead, but there is no reason to live in a state of paranoia either.

My family and I live in earthquake country, so we cannot afford *not* to prepare. I cannot say that my family and I would be able to go without outside food or water for an extended period, and I hope this capability will never be tested. However, we could probably make it for a period of days and perhaps weeks if there were no serious medical problems. We have canned food and bottled water, and we also have food ration bars, shelf-stable water boxes, and water filters for purifying standing water as well as other standard disaster supplies. Since I am a sprouter and a baker, an invaluable addition to our arsenal is a 5-gallon bucket of nitrogen-packed wheat grains plus a grain grinder, manual sprouter, and packets of yeast. When packed for long-term storage, wheat can last 10 years or longer, and can be ground into flour or coarse meal for simple pancakes, bread, or porridge. Kefir grains can do the same job as yeast, but it takes longer, and I prefer to have packets of yeast on hand just for emergencies. The live wheat grains also can be sprouted for their grass, which can either be chewed or juiced with a manual juicer for its green vegetable nutrition. Speaking of vegetable nutrition, there is no way you can grow extra vegetables on such short notice for an emergency, but sprouting extra vegetables only takes a few days. We also have a few long-term-storage packed cans of alfalfa and mung bean seeds, which both make extremely nutritious sprouts that can be eaten raw. For balanced protein, the mung beans also could be ground with the wheat and added to a porridge. You could continue adding additional stored grains, beans, and salad sprout seeds to cover you for any length of time, as well as additional long-term-packed foodstuffs such as honey, powdered milk, and salt. For sprouting seeds and long-term-storage packed food items, I highly recommend Walton Feed (www .waltonfeed.com), USA Emergency Supply (www.usaemergencysupply .com), and AAOOB Foods (www.aaoobfoods.com) as good places to start. Also keep tools nearby that are capable of opening sealed bucket lids and cans.

As we get within a year or two of the expiration dates on the wheat, sprouting seeds, and canned food, we rotate these into our food supply and replace them with newer storage seeds. Extra cooking oil and items such as dried fruit need to be rotated into use more often because they do not last as long. As the military food rations and shelf-stable water expire, we will junk them and get more, since I have no desire to integrate these into dinner as long as we have fresh food and water available. Store your supplies in buckets or large watertight plastic containers, which are also good to have on hand for transporting water or serving as makeshift toilets, if the need occurs.

Since water is essential to life, we can all hope that there is enough of it for everyone in the future. But for much of the western United States, Australia, New Zealand, and other places, water rationing may become par for the course. Since city residents generally do not have access to land for wells, springs, or streams, any water disruption may force you to locate, transport, and purify some standing water. One thing to remember is that most water heaters store some water in their tanks, and even if the tap runs dry, you may able to manually bleed the heater's tank using its overflow valve. In dry climates, there are some other ways to plan as well. If you have access to your building's roof or gutter drainage pipes, you can construct a simple rain barrel catchment system to bank water for future nonrainy days. You also can begin to use graywater (reused household water) to irrigate your vegetable garden, rather than pouring it down the drain.

Plan to invest in a good water filter or two (not the kind they sell at the drugstore for purifying tap water, but the kind they sell at a camping store for purifying lake or river water) so you will be able to purify any standing water or brackish water that you need to scavenge. You need not get an oil-drum-sized purifier. Thanks to improvements in technology, filtering water bottles (about $30 with one replaceable filter that purifies around 25 gallons) and even filtering straws (about $9, purifies 20 gallons) can allow you to drink directly from fetid, standing puddles of water and be assured of clean water with 99.99 percent of the harmful bacteria removed. Internet sources include Envirotech Products (www.envirotechproducts.com), Cabela's (www.cabelas.com), and REI (www.rei.com). A slightly larger Katadyn or MSR water purifier of the type sold to hikers and campers starts at around $60 and will purify 200 or more gallons on a single filter. Another option is to keep some iodine on hand; three drops per quart of water will decontaminate it within 20 minutes, and iodine can also disinfect wounds. The 10 percent iodine tinctures sold in drugstores are generally adequate for both purposes.

HIGH-CARB GARDENING

What if tough times continued for a while and you needed to garden not only for vegetables but also for your family's very survival? You might need to find a way to expand the size of your garden, which could include covering a patio, sidewalk, or driveway with dirt and putting in a survivalist planting of high-calorie food. Please refer to the section on sheet mulching and layered gardening starting on p. 139, where I explain a method for creating a very rich garden bed on a concrete surface. Other ways to expand your garden might be to appropriate a lawn, get permission to borrow someone else's yard, or acquire some larger containers to plant in.

The subject then becomes what to plant in order to sustain you and your family with the calories, as well as nutrition, that you might need for a period of time. You and your family cannot be self-sufficient unless you can farm several thousand square feet, but at least you can provide some of the survival food your family needs, and with proper storage it might last you well during tough times. Faced with this situation, my first advice would be to turn to sprouting in a really big way, because you could provide for a lot of your family's vegetable nutrition this way, while saving precious garden space for high-carb crops such as potatoes, grain, or corn. That said, we now turn to the high-calorie crops themselves.

Growing grain such as wheat, rye, barley, or oats is not as efficient as you might think, and it takes a lot of labor if you do it by hand. Rice and wild rice are both very water-intensive, which rules them out in many areas. You could try corn, but it is not all that productive for the space it uses, and getting the corn to wind-pollinate properly is sometimes diffi-cult with a small-sized planting. You may want to try growing a stand of grain or a few rows of corn to add to your food supply, but don't expect to feed your family this way unless you have lots of space and the means to harvest, thresh or shuck, dry, and store the grain properly. None of this is realistically possible on a meaningful scale for city gardeners. Fortunately, there is a better survivalist crop out there.

The potato produces more calories and protein than any other food crop in terms of space and amount of time. It also stores for up to six months under good conditions and can be grown in marginal soil anywhere from sea level up to 13,000 feet. The potato produces about 10,000 pounds of food per acre.[111] A 100-foot row can yield 150 to 300 pounds of potatoes per year.[112] The average American currently eats about 140 pounds of potatoes per year, while just before the Irish potato famine, with potatoes as the country's main food staple, the average Irish person was eating 10 pounds a day (equating to 3,650 pounds per year).[113] But although this might seem an intimidating amount to grow in any urban space, even a container-based garden can yield enough spuds to provide your family with enough to eat for days on end. Salvaging some garbage cans, drilling drainage holes in the bottom, and filling them with dirt plus seed potatoes, would probably yield around 20 pounds of spuds per garbage can. You also can use spare tires as bedding frames or, as indicated earlier, start a sheet-mulched bed directly on concrete. Potatoes like to grow upward, and will produce more heavily if they do, so standard practice for most growers is to mound up material over the plants as they grow, forcing them to grow taller and add another level of tubers underneath. This mounding material can be soil or any mulch, so even an incomplete sheet-mulched bed may be adequate for potatoes (though, to limit the possibility of disease, I would surround the seed potatoes with a layer of soil or peat rather than rotting material).

Ideally, you should start with certified disease-free potatoes for seeding, but in a pinch you can also chop up chunks of your own potatoes, provided they do not show any signs of disease. Pick the healthiest-looking ones, and cut them into small golf-ball-sized pieces, making sure there is at least one eye in each.[114] You can either green-sprout them, as many Europeans do, which involves putting the spuds on a sunny windowsill to sprout before planting, or you can simply plant them and they should sprout underground. Potatoes germinate when the soil temperature is between 45 and 50 degrees F, meaning that in many parts of North America they can be grown nearly year-round. In slightly colder locations, they will grow (or store underground) during much of the year, particularly with a protective mulching of straw, burlap, or newspaper if needed. Of course, you also could dig them up and store them indoors to prevent damage from vermin and colder temperatures.

It would be nice if none of us had to worry about resource shortages. People who grew up during the Great Depression or survived tough wartime conditions in other countries do not take for granted the things that later generations have come to expect as our rights. But with the rapidly increasing cost of food and energy, and the likelihood that the days of cheap resources are nearing their end, there may well be periods of time when some items are rationed, in short supply, or simply prohibitively expensive, even without any natural disasters. Whatever the reason, it is good to be well prepared with short-term backup sources of energy, water, and food. And I hope that your greatest benefit from reading this chapter is that it will encourage you to improve your skills in sprouting, begin buying some basic foods in bulk, learn to grow spuds, ultimately moving a little closer to sustainability living, even in good times.

thirteen

HELPING TO BUILD
A SUSTAINABLE FUTURE

In an ideal world, humanity would use renewable sources of energy, our economic system would work in harmony with the natural world around us, we would practice organic methods of agriculture, and everyone would get along with one another. If there is a silver lining to the problems of global warming and diminishing energy resources, it is that we finally may be forced to work together toward some common global solutions. Unfortunately, you and I cannot exercise much control over public policy or private business decisions from the top down. But we can, and must, effect change from the ground up.

In the last two decades, farmers' markets have spread across North America as country and city have come together for a weekly celebration of the ongoing harvest. City residents can buy fresh food, talk to the people who have grown it, see the dirt on their hands, and feel temporarily satisfied that they are buying and eating real food. Small family farmers gain a direct outlet for their produce, meet the people who are buying and consuming it, and feel some pride in presenting these city residents with the fruits of their labor and land. In my mind, farmers' markets are a strong indication that there is a hunger in the city for something more meaningful than a drive to the grocery store for plastic food. And a lot of people are willing to pay higher prices for farmers' market fare.

As demand for organic products has skyrocketed in recent years, people who can afford it have clearly signaled their willingness to pay more for better stuff. What most people do not realize is that the price of organic and farmers' market produce is much closer to the *real* cost of that food. Residents of Europe and industrialized Asia are accustomed to paying more for their food than we normally do. In the United States, food is comparatively cheap. Or is it? Consider the following statement from Francis Moore Lappe, author of *Diet for a Small Planet*:

"We've actually let market prices lie to us. They don't register all the hidden costs of our 'factory farming' model, costs that undermine the very sustainability of nature's gifts. Food prices don't count the fact that soil is eroding on prime farmland many times faster than nature rebuilds it, or the marine life we're losing because of nitrogen runoff from overusing fertilizers. . . . The prices don't include the loss of plant diversity that occurs when our seed is supplied by just a few companies aggressively marketing a limited selection, or when the wells in Midwest states are poisoned by farm chemicals. Eating it adds a host of additional costs, including more than 5,000 deaths each year from food-borne illnesses, even as agribusiness—especially the meat industry—has fought against adding the cost of stricter food safety procedures to the bottom line. We've boasted that ours is the world's most efficient food system, but no business could stay afloat for long while ignoring its real costs. Efficiency and sustainability—the maintenance of Earth's gifts to us and our health over time—can no longer be seen as contradictory aims."[115]

And this is just the beginning. The true cost of food in the United States should also factor in how much it costs to transport our meals from field to plate. Each year, the American taxpayers spend billions of dollars on huge subsidies for highways, bridges, harbors, and airports; without this infrastructure, small local farmers would be on an equal (or better) footing compared to the multinational food producers whose products are imported from foreign countries, where labor and environmental standards are looser than ours.[116] Then there are the agricultural subsidies that our government hands out each year. Although these benefit a few small family farmers, they increasingly have become a corporate handout for large agribusinesses. According to a study by the conservative Heritage Foundation, the top 10 largest and richest "farmers" received some 73 percent of the $171 billion in farm subsidies given over a 10-year period.[117] Among the top 10 recipients were several Fortune 500 companies, which were mostly paid taxpayer dollars to grow plenty of corn, soybeans, and meat in the Midwest that could be shipped overseas at artificially competitive prices.[118]

Also consider how much energy it takes to grow and transport our food. In April 2006, with the price of gasoline at about $3 per gallon in the U.S., Milton Copulos, President of the National Defense Council Foundation and Senior Fellow at the Institute for the Analysis of Global Security, gave testimony before the U.S. Senate Foreign Relations Committee regarding his analysis of the actual cost of gasoline. He testified that the full price of a gallon of gasoline for the U.S. taxpayer, figuring in the cost of military security in the Persian Gulf, should be closer to $10 per gallon.[119] In May 2006, *Sierra* magazine ran an article breaking down how far your food travels and how much energy this requires. (See the following chart, which assumes that the consumer buys the food item in Des Moines, Iowa.)

INPUT DISTANCES TRAVELED BY PRODUCE AND MODE OF TRANSPORT, FROM SOURCE TO DES MOINES FOOD STORE:

- Apple (Iowa)—60 miles by light truck (gas)
- Apple (Washington)—1,722 miles by commercial truck (diesel)
- Grapes (California)—1,887 miles by commercial truck (diesel)
- Grapes (Chile)—5,585 miles by ship (residual fuel oil); 1,683 miles by commercial truck (diesel)
- Potato (North Dakota)—558 miles by commercial truck (diesel)
- Potato (Idaho)—1,246 miles by commercial truck (diesel)
- Pineapple (Costa Rica)—1,211 miles by ship (residual fuel oil); 1,466 miles by commercial truck (diesel)
- Pineapple (Hawaii)—2,551 miles by plane (kerosene jet fuel); 1,683 miles by commercial truck (diesel). (Only specialty Hawaiian pineapples are shipped by air. Most come in the same fashion as the Costa Rican fruit, by sea and truck.)

VOLUME OF FUEL NEEDED TO TRANSPORT PRODUCE:

- Apple (Iowa)—0.048 ounces (0.288 teaspoons)
- Apple (Washington)—0.96 ounces (5.76 teaspoons)
- One-pound bunch of grapes (California)—1.76 ounces (3.5 tablespoons)
- One-pound bunch of grapes (Chile)—2.1 ounces (4.2 tablespoons)
- Potato (North Dakota)—0.52 ounces (1 tablespoon)
- Potato (Idaho)—1.12 ounces (2.25 tablespoons)

• Pineapple (Costa Rica)—4.32 ounces (0.54 cup)

• Pineapple (Hawaii)—67.68 ounces (0.529 gallons)

Figures from Sierra magazine.[120]

If you want to, you can calculate the real cost of an apple or potato. But more importantly, you can understand how our system has made mass-produced and imported food seem much cheaper than it really ought to be. You also can imagine how a continuing increase in oil prices will make transported food difficult to afford anyway.

When you buy locally produced, organic food, and it costs more money than the plastic food in the stores, this is closer to its real cost. By buying local and organic, you are immediately paying the environmental and nutritional premium for renewing the land, a bill that will come due much later for the poisoned tracts of agribusiness land and the consumers who suffer from chronic diseases that largely could be prevented by better nutrition.

Pay more for local, organic produce. Build up the soil in your own garden; nothing is more local, organic, or nutritious than what you can grow yourself. Your wealth is in this soil and in the skills you can apply to help you produce food from a home garden, chicken coop, mushroom box, sprouting bin, or any other source. Learn the skills you'll need to make a difference in your own life and in your family's health and well being. And share what you learn with others.

As you share your knowledge with family, friends, and neighbors, they can become empowered also. Perhaps your building has no yard that belongs to you but a large lawn that is maintained by a landlord or homeowners' association. Lawns are a poor use of resources and a space that can be better utilized.[121] What if a group of homeowners in the building makes a push for using that land for growing vegetables or raising chickens? One person volunteers to set it up and others pitch in. Perhaps the city's zoning laws do not permit chickens or open compost piles in a multiunit complex and so the building residents band together and present the city council with their reasons for changing the law. A small community farm is born, and residents of the building have access to fresh eggs and salad greens all year long in exchange for a few work hours or a membership fee. As they share their good fortune with friends, other buildings in the neighborhood and city put the same model into practice. Soon the developers know a good thing when they see one, and new building plans with integrated community farms start to be developed. Residents produce some of their own food locally, soil is improved, and people start to get along with one another as they work together with a common interest. And as with farmers' markets, this model spreads to the state, country, and beyond. Other cities see what is happening and decide to encourage better use of the land, so they provide tax breaks for building owners and residents to start small community farms. Some even provide space for community gardens and composting sites. Then the state, and the country, and . . . .

Can we really change the world from the ground up? Take it from some folks who started small. Mahatma Gandhi said, "You must be the change you want to see in the world." And Margaret Mead said, "Never doubt that a small group of thoughtful, committed citizens can change the world. Indeed, it's the only thing that ever has." We each have a part to play, and it begins with our own lives. I will leave you with one more quote from Confucius and then let you pursue your own path:

> When things are investigated, then true knowledge is achieved;
> When true knowledge is achieved, then the will becomes sincere;
> When the will is sincere, then the heart is set right;
> When the heart is set right, then the personal life is cultivated;
> When the personal life is cultivated, then the family life is
>   regulated;
> When the family life is regulated, then the national life is orderly;
> And when the national life is orderly, then there is peace in the
>   world.[122]

NOTES

1. Deffeyes, Kenneth S., *Hubbert's Peak: The Impending World Oil Shortage* (Princeton, NJ: Princeton University Press, 2001), 1.

2. Simmons, Matthew, *Twilight in the Desert: The Coming Saudi Oil Shock and the World Economy* (Hoboken, NJ: Wiley, 2005), 343.

3. Baker, David R., "Chevron campaign tries to balance need for oil with global warming," *San Francisco Chronicle* (September 28, 2007): C1.

4. Leeb, Stephen, *The Coming Economic Collapse: How You Can Thrive When Oil Costs $200 a Barrel* (New York: Warner Business Books, 2006), 2.

5. Deffeyes (see note 1), 1.

6. "Biofuels may threaten environment, UN warns," CNN (January 23, 2008). Article available online at www.cnn.com/2008/TECH/science/01/23/biofuels.fears.ap/index.html (visited January 26, 2008).

7. Johnson, Robbin S., and C. Ford Runge, "Ethanol: Train Wreck Ahead?" *Issues in Science and Technology* 24:1 (September 22, 2006): 25–26.

8. U.S. Census Bureau. Population Trends in Metropolitan and Micropolitan Statistical Areas: 1999–2003. Population Estimates and Projections (September 2005).

9. U.S. Department of Agriculture, National Agricultural Statistics Service. Trends in U.S. Agriculture. Available online at www.usda.gov/nass/pubs/trends/index.htm (visited January 21, 2008).

10. Flottum, Kim, *The Backyard Beekeeper: An Absolute Beginner's Guide to Keeping Bees in Your Yard and Garden* (Beverly, MA: Quarry Books, 2005), 12.

11. Weinmann, Todd, *Companion Planting*. Cass County Extension, North Dakota State University Extension (updated May 2002).

12. Reeves, Carrie, *Companion Planting Improves Gardens*, Mississippi State University, Office of Agricultural Publishing (August 27, 2001).

13. Weinmann (see note 11).

14. Riotte, Louise, *Carrots Love Tomatoes: Secrets of Companion Planting for Successful Gardening* (Pownal, VT: Storey Publishing, 1998), 2.

15. Weinmann (see note 11).

16. Beyfuss, Robert, and Marvin Pritts, "Cornell gardening resources: companion planting." Cornell University Department of Horticulture, Cooperative Extension. EcoGardening Fact Sheet #10 (Winter 1994, updated September 2006).

17. Riotte (see note 14).

18. Coleman, Eliot, *Four-Season Harvest: Organic Vegetables from Your Home Garden All Year Long* (White River Junction, VT: Chelsea Green Publishing, 1999), 139–141.

19. Ibid.

20. Ibid.

21. Jones, K. S., and Laurence R. Costello, *Selecting Fruit, Nut, and Berry Crops for Home Gardens in San Mateo and San Francisco Counties*, University of California Division of Agriculture and Natural Resources, Publication Number 8261, 4.

22. Sauls, Julian, and Larry K. Jackson, "Growing Fruit Crops in Containers." Florida Cooperative Extension Service, Institute of Food and Agriculture Science, University of Florida, Fruit Crops Fact Sheet FC-57.

23. Hauser, Kevin, *Growing Apples in the City* (Riverside, CA: Kuffel Creek Press, 2007). This title is available as an e-book through the author's Web site, www.kuffelcreek.com.

24. Anderson, Peter C., and Timothy Crocker, *Low Chill Apple Cultivars for North and North Central Florida*, Florida Cooperative Extension Service, Institute of Food and Agriculture Science, University of Florida, Horticultural Sciences Department Publication HS764.

25. Poling, E. B., *Raspberries in the Home Garden*, North Carolina Cooperative Extension Service, North Carolina State University. Horticulture Information Leaflet 8204.

26. Merten, Sven, "A Review of Hylocereus Production in the United States," *Journal of the Professional Association for Cactus Development* 5 (2003): 98–105.

27. "Fig Culture in Northern Climates," Cornell Cooperative Extension, Nassau County, New York. Home Grounds Fact Sheet.

28. "Jujube: Fruit Facts," California Rare Fruit Growers. Publication available online from this organization's Web site at www.crfg.org/pubs/ff/jujube.html (visited January 10, 2008).

29. Morton, Julia, *Fruits of Warm Climates*. (Miami: Florida Fair Books, 1987), 293–300.

30. Perry, Leonard, *Garden Mazes and Labyrinths*, University of Vermont Extension, Department of Plant and Soil Science. Publication OH-74 (revised June 2002).

31. Peirce, Pam, *Golden Gate Gardening: The Complete Guide to Year-round Food Gardening in the San Francisco Bay Area and California* (Seattle, WA: Sasquatch Books, 1998), 335–36.

32. Schalau, Jeff. "Growing Persimmons." Arizona Cooperative Extension, Yavapai County. *Backyard Gardener Newsletter* (January 7, 2004).

33. Olsen, Jeff, and Robert L. Stebbins, *Growing Tree Fruits and Nuts in the Home Orchard*. Oregon State University Extension Service. Publication EC 819 (revised December 2007).

34. Kinion, Jennifer, "Beautiful, Exotic Pineapple Guava." *Marin Independent Journal* (May 6, 2006). This article is available online at www.marinij.com/lifestyles/ci_3790580.

35. Peirce (see note 31), 333–34.

36. Facciola, Stephen, *Cornucopia: A Source Book of Edible Plants* (Vista, CA: Kampong Publications, 1990), 380.

37. "Loquat: Fruit Facts," California Rare Fruit Growers. Publication available online from this organization's Web site at http://www.crfg.org/pubs/ff/loquat.html (visited December 30, 2007).

38. Funt, Richard C., "Plums: A Guide to Selection and Use," Ohio State University Extension Fact Sheet HYG 1404–92.

39. Trevino, Laramie, "Intensive Effort Creates Orchard in Any Backyard: High Density Planting Can Yield Months of Fresh Fruit from Impossibly Small Spaces," *San Francisco Chronicle* (February 4, 2004). Article available online at http://www.sfgate.com/cgi-bin/article.cgi?file=/c/a/2004/02/04/HOGHM4N75K1.DTL.

40. Marini, Richard, *Growing Apples in Virginia*, Virginia Cooperative Extension. Publication 422–023 (July 1996).

41. Lord, William G. *Choosing the Right Apple Rootstock*, University of New Hampshire Cooperative Extension (Revised February 2001).

42. Allen, Oliver A. *Gardening with the New Small Plants* (Boston: Houghton Mifflin, 1987), 149–51.

43. Slingerland, Ken, Bill Lay, and David Hunter, "Pear Cultivars." Ontario Ministry of Agriculture, Food and Rural Affairs. Factsheet 02–039 (August 2002).

44. Laivo, Ed, "Blueberries in Containers." Article available online at the Dave Wilson Nursery Web site, http://www.davewilson.com/homegrown/promotion/bluecontainer.html. (visited January 2, 2007).

45. Thayer, Samuel, *The Forager's Harvest: A Guide to Identifying, Harvesting, and Preparing Edible Wild Plants* (Ogema, WI: Forager's Harvest Publishing, 2006).

46. Hauser (see note 23), 82.

47. Otto, Stella, *The Backyard Berry Book: A Hands-On Guide to Growing Berries, Brambles, and Vine Fruit in the Home Garden* (Maple City, MI: Ottographics, 1995), 189–203.

48. Foulk, Doug S., and Emily E. Hoover, *Currants and Gooseberries in the Home Garden*, University of Minnesota Extension Service. Publication FS-01122 (revised 1998).

49. Joyce, David, and Christopher Brickell, *The Complete Guide to Pruning and Training Plants* (New York: Simon & Schuster/Mitchell Beazley Publishers, 1992).

50. Greene, Janet, Ruth Hertzberg, and Beatrice Vaughan, *Putting Food By* (Lexington, MA: The Stephen Greene Press, 1988).

51. The Gardeners and Farmers of Terre Vivante, *Preserving Food Without Freezing or Canning* (White River Junction, VT: Chelsea Green Publishing, 2007).

52. Ball, Jeff, *The Self-Sufficient Suburban Garden* (Emmaus, PA: Rodale Press, 1983), 97.

53. Thayer (see note 45).

54. Meyerowitz, Steve, "This Winter and This Millennium, Don't Forget the Sprouts. Good Sprout News," Fact Sheet produced by International Sprout Growers Association. Available online at www.isga-sprouts.org/nutrit1.htm (visited February 22, 2008).

55. Mitchell, Deborah. *The Broccoli Sprouts Breakthrough* (New York: St. Martin's Press, 1998), 86–87. Also see Anne M. Kylen and Rolland M. McCready, "Nutrients in seeds and sprouts of alfalfa, lentils, mung beans, and soybeans," *Journal of Food Science* 40:5 (1975): 1008–9.

56. United States Department of Agriculture, Agricultural Research Service, Nutrient Data Laboratory. National Nutrient Database for Standard Reference. "Soybean sprouts, cooked, stir-fried." Database available at www.nal.usda.gov/fnic/foodcomp/search (visited January 10, 2008).

57. Mitchell (see note 55).

58. United States Department of Agriculture, Agricultural Research Service, Nutrient Data Laboratory. National Nutrient Database for Standard Reference. "Alfalfa seeds, sprouted, raw." Database available at www.nal.usda.gov/fnic/foodcomp/search (visited January 10, 2008).

59. Kurtzer, M. S., and X. Xu, "Dietary Phytoestrogens," *Annual Review of Nutrition* 17 (1997): 353–81. Digest of article provided on the following Web site: www.isga-sprouts.org/alfalfa.htm (visited February 22, 2008).

60. Broccoli Sprouts Eaten During Pregnancy May Provide Children with Life-Long Protection Against Heart Disease. University of Saskatchewan. Press release issued January 31, 2006.

61. Lopez-Otsoa, F., A. Rementeria, N. Elguezabal, and J. Garaizar, "Kefir: A symbiotic yeast-bacteria community with alleged healthy capabilities," *Revista Iberoamericana de Micología* 23 (2006): 67–74.

62. Katz, Sandor Ellix, *Wild Fermentation: The Flavor, Nutrition, and Craft of Live-Culture Foods* (White River Junction, VT: Chelsea Green Publishing, 2003), 79–80.

63. Lopez-Otsoa (see note 61). Also see S. Salminen, C. Bouley, and M. Boutron-Ruault, "Functional food science and gastrointestinal physiology and function," *British Journal of Nutrition* 80 (1998): S147–71.

64. Raymond, Joan, "World's Healthiest Foods: Kimchi," *Health* (March 2006). Article available online at www.health.com/health/article/0,23414,1149143,00.html (visited February 22, 2008).

65. Sanders, Mary Ellen, "Probiotics, strains matter," *Functional Foods and Nutraceuticals Magazine*(June 2007): 36–41.

66. Tucker, Miriam, "The good bugs," *Boston Globe* (November 21, 2000): E1.

67. Goulart, Frances Sheridan, *Super Healing Foods.* (Englewood Cliffs, NJ: Prentice Hall, 1995), 271.

68. Katz (see note 62).

69. Stamets, Paul, *Growing Gourmet and Medicinal Mushrooms* (Berkeley, CA: Ten Speed Press, 2000); Paul Stamets and J. S. Chilton, *The Mushroom Cultivator: A Practical Guide to Growing Mushrooms at Home* (Olympia, WA: Agarikon Press, 1983).

70. Lee, Andy, and Pat Foreman, *Chicken Tractor: The Permaculture Guide to Happy Hens and Healthy Soil* (Buena Vista, VA: Good Earth Publications, 1998).

71. Damerow, Gail. *Barnyard in Your Backyard* (North Adams, MA: Storey Publishing, 2002, 27.

72. Lyons, Jesse J., *Small Flock Series: Managing a Family Chicken Flock*, University of Missouri Extension. Publication G8350 (February 1997).

73. Long, Cheryl, "Portable Chicken Mini-Coop," *Mother Earth News* (April/May 2007). Article available in the *Mother Earth News* archive at www.motherearthnews.com/DIY/2007–04–01/Portable-Chicken-Mini-coop-Plan.aspx.

74. Damerow (see note 71), 29.

75. Hamre, Melvin L., *The Small Laying Flock*, University of Minnesota Extension. Publication FS-01192 (reviewed 1998).

76. Damerow (see note 71), 29.

77. Lyons (see note 72); Damerow (see note 71), 31–32.

78. Damerow (see note 71), 31–32.

79. Ibid., 30–32.

80. Lyons (see note 72).

81. Hamre (see note 75).

82. Lyons (see note 72).

83. Flottum (see note 10), 12.

84. Paulson, Amanda, "Plants, grass on the rooftop? No longer an oddity." *Christian Science Monitor* (July 10, 2006).

85. Hume, Marion, "What's the Buzz?" Time/CNN (November 21, 2007).

86. Flottum (see note 10), 16.

87. Ibid., 10.

88. Conrad, Ross, *Natural Beekeeping: Organic Approaches to Modern Apiculture* (White River Junction, VT: Chelsea Green Publishing, 2007).

89. Whiting, David, Adrian Card, and Carl Wilson, "Using Manure in the Home Garden," Colorado State University Extension. GardenNotes #242 (revised December 2006).

90. Garrett, Howard. The Dirt Doctor: Natural and Organic Products Database: Rabbit manure. Available online at www.dirtdoctor.com (visited January 14, 2008).

91. United States Environmental Protection Agency. Composting: Environmental Benefits. Fact sheet available online at www.epa.gov/epaoswer/non-hw/composting/benefits.htm. Page updated September 7, 2007 (visited January 3, 2008).

92. Pleasant, Barbara, "Compost Made Easy," *Mother Earth News* (October/November 2006). Article available online via the *Mother Earth News* archive at www.motherearthnews.com/Organic-Gardening/2006–10–01/Compost-Made-Easy.aspx.

93. Solomon, Steve, *Gardening When It Counts: Growing Food in Hard Times* (Gabriola Island, BC: New Society Publishers, 2005), 200–201.

94. Pleasant (see note 92).

95. Ibid.

96. Dean, Esther, *Esther Dean's Gardening Book: Gardening Without Digging* (Sydney: Harper & Row, 1977).

97. Fukuoka, Masanobu, *One-Straw Revolution: An Introduction to Natural Farming* (Emmaus, PA: Rodale Press, 1978).

98. Lanza, Patricia, *Lasagna Gardening* (Emmaus, PA: Rodale Press, 1998).

99. Scott, Nicky, *Composting: An Easy Household Guide* (White River Junction, VT: Chelsea Green Publishing, 2007).

100. Elliott, Brook, "Compost Tumblers," *Mother Earth News* (April/May 2003). Article available online via the *Mother Earth News* archive at www.motherearthnews.com/Nature-and-Environment/2003–04–01/Compost-Tumblers.aspx.

101. Ball (see note 52), 146.

102. Solomon (see note 93), 208–209.

103. Gillard, Spring, *Diary of a Compost Hotline Operator: Edible Essays on City Farming* (Gabriola Island, BC: New Society Publishers, 2003).

104. Elcock, Gillian, and Josie Martens, *Composting with Red Wiggler Worms*, Urban Agriculture Notes, City Farmer. Canada Office of Urban Agriculture (published 1995). This guide is available online from the City Farmer Web site at www.cityfarmer.org/wormcomp61.html#wormcompost.

105. Appelhof, Mary, *Worms Eat My Garbage: How to Set Up & Maintain a Worm Composting System* (Kalamazoo, MI: Flower Press, 1997).

106. Appelhof, Mary, "Let Worms Eat Your Garbage," *Mother Earth News* (July/August 1983). Article available online via the *Mother Earth News* archive at www.motherearthnews.com/Whole-Foods-and-Cooking/1983–07–01/Let-Worms-Eat-Your-Garbage.aspx.

107. Stewart, Amy, *The Earth Moved: On the Remarkable Achievements of Earthworms* (Chapel Hill, NC: Algonquin Books of Chapel Hill, 2005).

108. McBay, Aric, *Peak Oil Survival: Preparation for Life After Gridcrash.* (Guilford, CT: The Lyons Press, 2006).

109. Heinberg, Richard, *Peak Everything: Waking Up to the Century of Declines* (Gabriola Island, BC: New Society Publishers, 2007).

110. Manjoo, Farhad, Page Rockwell, and Aaron Kinney, "Timeline to disaster." Salon.com (September 15, 2005). Article available online at dir.salon.com/story/news/feature/2005/09/15/katrina_timeline/index.html?pn=1 (visited January 16, 2008).

111. Hollingsworth, Dave, "Growing Potatoes Organically: Basics from Seed to Storage," University of California, Vegetable Research and Information Center. No publication date or document number available. Document available online at vric.ucdavis.edu/veginfo/commodity/potato/organic_potatoes.pdf (visited February 24, 2008).

112. Pack, Jeffery, James M. White, and Chad M. Hutchinson, *Growing Potatoes in the Florida Home Garden,* Florida Cooperative Extension Service, Horticultural Sciences Department, University of Florida. Publication HS933 (July 2003).

113. Northern Plains Potato Growers Association. Some fun stuff on potatoes. Fact sheet available at www.rrvpotatoes.org/consumer-facts.htm ((visited January 16, 2008).

114. Pack (see note 112).

115. Lappe, Frances Moore, and Anna Lappe, "Dispel the Myth that Cheap Food Comes Without High Costs," *Los Angeles Times* (April 18, 2002). Frances Moore Lappe's full book is *Diet For a Small Planet* (New York: Ballantine Books, 1991).

116. Waite, Hardly, "How Much Does Food Really Cost?" *Pure Water Gazette.* Article available online at www.purewatergazette.net/costoffood.htm (visited January 17, 2008).

117. Reidl, Brian, "Still at the Federal Trough: Farm Subsidies for the Rich and Famous Shattered Records in 2001," The Heritage Foundation, Backgrounder #1542 (April 30, 2002).

118. Lappe (see note 115); Waite (see note 116).

119. Testimony of Milton R. Copulos before the Senate Foreign Relations Committee (March 30, 2006). Transcript available from the Senate Foreign Relations Committee's Web site at foreign.senate.gov/testimony/2006/CopulosTestimony060330.pdf.

120. Rauber, Paul, "Decoder: Miles to Go Before You Eat," *Sierra* (May 31, 2006).

121. Flores, Heather Coburn, *Food Not Lawns: How to Turn Your Yard into a Garden and Your Neighborhood into a Community* (White River Junction, VT: Chelsea Green, 2006).

122. Bartleby.com, Reference, Quotations. Available online at www.bartleby.com (visited January 17, 2008).

RESOURCES

TOOLS, SOIL AMENDMENTS, AND VARIOUS SUPPLIES

Heavy items are best purchased locally, if you can find them, because you will pay a lot more with shipping. Nevertheless, some things are not available locally at the right price or level of quality, so here are some good mail order sources, which also have informative Internet sites.

Composters. The name says it all—this site sells many sizes and shapes of composters and compost bins. Whether you buy here or elsewhere, this is a great place to start so that you can see some of the possibilities before purchasing anything. www.composters.com

Craigslist. A little less well-known than eBay, Craigslist is basically the world's largest collection of classified ads. You can search by location as well as by item, and you even can search the personal ads for other people interested in growing food. By its nature, Craigslist requires a bit of a buyer-beware approach, but it still can be a good resource. www.craigslist.org

Earthbox. Well-made self-watering planter boxes that are big enough to grow quality vegetables. www.earthbox.com

eBay. When you can't find something anywhere else, you can always try eBay. Buyer beware: You are dealing with a lot of amateur sellers, so seeds, plants, and other merchandise are not always what they seem. In recent years, I've purchased some things on eBay that I had a hard time finding elsewhere, such as yacon bulbs (edible, perennial root), a used compost tumbler in great shape, and plant seeds during the off-season. But I admit that I've also wasted money on some real junk. Nevertheless, if you're looking for a hard-to-find item or something that's out-of-season elsewhere, this is one place to keep an eye on. www.ebay.com

Freecycle. An online network of people, organized into groups by location, who are giving away and getting things, all for free. Someone just might have what you want, and they don't want it, and there you go. www.freecycle.org

Gardener's Supply. This Vermont-based company sells growing containers, composters, garden tools, and more. They have a growing array of self-watering planters. Their merchandise is not cheap, but it's generally good quality and sometimes hard to find elsewhere. www.gardeners.com

Gardens Alive. Eco-friendly gardening products. Sells a number of organic soil amendments, but is most useful for its array of environmentally friendly pest control products. www.gardensalive.com

Lee Valley Tools. High quality, long-lasting tools are hard to find these days, yet few things are more essential for sustainable living. This is one of the most reliable mail order sources in the business. www.leevalley.com

Marshall Grain Company. Texas-based feed store that carries a lot of organic gardening items at very reasonable prices, even considering the added cost of shipping. Good selection of organic soil amendments and pest controls. www.marshallgrain.com

Peaceful Valley Farm & Garden Supply. Fantastic resource for organic gardeners. Carries everything from vegetable seeds and fruit trees to organic fertilizers and composting supplies. Beginning gardeners also should check out the tools section, which has some excellent hand tools for small-scale gardening. www.groworganic.com

Pleasant Hill Grain. Reliable source of big-ticket kitchen items such as grain mills, dehydrators, fruit presses, water purifiers, and more. With these larger kitchen items, you get what you pay for, yet these folks sell durable brands at reasonable prices. www.pleasanthillgrain.com

VEGETABLE SEED SUPPLIERS

All of these companies will ship mail order seeds via Internet order or catalog. My choices here are informed both by my own experience and, for some of the companies outside my region, by Steve Solomon's advice in his book *Gardening When It Counts* (see note 93). Based on his experience in the seed business, he maintains that many of the larger seed catalogs sell their best stuff to large-scale farmers, and that home gardeners often get the dregs. The three largest ones listed here (Johnny's, Harris, and Park) get his stamp of approval.

Evergreen Seeds (California). Small seed retailer that stocks Asian vegetable seeds. You will find vegetables here that are available nowhere else. They have a large selection of oriental greens, as well as more than a dozen varieties each of daikon radishes and of Japanese and Korean cucumbers. www.evergreenseeds.com

Fedco Seeds (Maine). Seed co-op that provides untreated vegetable seeds that are particularly well-suited for the Northeast. Their Moose Tubers section also sells seed potatoes, onion sets, and sunchokes. www.fedcoseeds.com

Harris Seeds (New York). Another large seed company with a long history. Their vegetable varieties are particularly well-suited for the Northeast and Midwest. www.harrisseeds.com

High Mowing Organic Seeds (Vermont). A reputable source for certified organic seeds. Like Victory Seed Company below, they emphasize open-pollinated seeds and heirloom varieties, along with modern and unique hybrids. www.highmowingseeds.com

Johnny's Selected Seeds (Maine). Among the best in the business. Offers very reliable vegetable seeds and a large selection. www.johnnyseeds.com

Park Seed (South Carolina). This retailer has a long tradition providing flower and vegetable seeds that will thrive in southern gardens and beyond. Park also has some useful seed-starting materials. www.parkseed.com

Renee's Garden (California). Small seed company offering the owner's hand-selected varieties of gourmet garden vegetables, flowers, and herbs, including open-pollinated, heirloom, and hybrid varieties. www.reneesgarden.com

Ronniger Potato Farm (Colorado). Ships hundreds of varieties of early season, mid-season, late season, and fingerling seed potatoes, as well as onions and garlic. Many organic spuds are available. www.ronnigers .com

Seed Savers Exchange (Iowa). This non-profit organization saves and maintains heirloom vegetable, fruit, flower, and herb seeds. Once you join as a member, you have access to many of the selections that are grown on its 23-acre certified organic garden. www.seedsavers.org

Territorial Seed (Oregon). Very high quality source of vegetable, flower, and herb seeds, particularly those that will succeed on the West Coast. Also carries natural and organic fertilizers, composting supplies, and tools. www.territorialseed.com

Victory Seed Company (Oregon). Sells open-pollinated, heirloom vegetable seeds. They farm and grow most of their own seed plants. www.victoryseeds.com.

Willhite Seed Company (Texas). These folks carry plenty of vegetable seeds that will thrive during humid summers. If you live in the South and have enough space, don't miss their watermelons. www.willhite seed.com

FRUIT TREE SUPPLIERS (MAIL ORDER)

Bay Laurel Nursery (California). Mail order supplier of bare root fruit trees. This site also has good information about different rootstocks for fruit trees and their varying attributes. www.baylaurelnursery.com

Hartmann's Plant Company (Michigan). This is a great place for berries of all sorts, including raspberries, blueberries, currants, and gooseberries. They have a particularly good selection of blueberries for both northern and southern climate gardeners. www.hartmanns plantcompany.com

Miller Nurseries (New York). Mail order supplier of bare root fruit trees and various berries, including many cold-hardy varieties including kiwis and paw-paws. www.millernurseries.com

Nourse Farms (Massachusetts). Quality retailer of berries for northern gardeners. Check out their thornless blackberries. Their website also breaks down the blueberries, raspberries, and strawberries into different categories based on when they ripen (early season, mid-season, late season, etc.), which can be very helpful if you want a prolonged harvest. www.noursefarms.com

One Green World (Oregon). This nursery searches the world for unique and unusual temperate fruits. If you'd like to try a Chilean Guava, Goji Berry, or Akebia Vine, this is the place. Also sells more recognizable temperate fruits. www.onegreenworld.com

Pine Island Nursery (Florida). Pine Island sells tropical fruit trees by mail order. If you live in a very warm climate or would like to experiment with something exotic under a bright sunny window, then this is a good source. They carry everything from avocados and cashew nuts to sapodillas and white sapotes, not to mention mangoes for every letter of the alphabet. www.tropicalfruitnursery.com

Raintree Nursery (Washington). This is a wonderful source for apple trees, many of them disease-resistant. They also sell many small and exotic fruits for temperate climates. They carry 800 varieties of fruits, berries, and unusual edibles. www.raintreenursery.com

Sandusky Valley Nursery (Ohio). Sandusky has a limited, but high quality, selection of fruit and nut trees. It includes some natives as well as temperate exotics. Cannot ship to some West Coast states. www.svnursery.com

Stark Brothers (Missouri). This nursery has a long tradition of supplying great fruit trees and berry bushes to home growers. Very impressive selection of dwarf fruit trees. www.starkbros.com

USEFUL INFORMATION

Association for the Study of Peak Oil & Gas (ASPO). "ASPO is a network of scientists and others, having an interest in determining the date and impact of the peak and decline of the world's production of oil and gas, due to resource constraints." This was once the only site devoted to peak oil information, but now there are dozens, maybe hundreds. For more information on this phenomenon, you also can do an Internet search for "peak oil" and see what other resources come up. www.peakoil.net

City Farmer. Urban gardeners and composters in Vancouver, Canada, have done an amazing job of sharing their stories and empowering others with information and encouragement. Visit this site and scroll down for a great compilation of useful guidance about composting and growing food in any city. www.cityfarmer.org

Energy Bulletin. A good, updated page of news related to energy, oil depletion, and the impact of rising prices. www.energybulletin.net

Local Harvest. Organic food website that helps you find local organic farmers, farmers' markets, and sustainably grown local food. This is a great resource and it's sure to become either a hub or a model for such information-sharing in the near future. www.localharvest.org

North American Fruit Explorers (NAFEX) and California Rare Fruit Growers (CRFG). NAFEX is a nationwide network of amateur fruit growers who share a common passion for growing fine, and often unusual, fruit. NAFEX also has regional chapters and interest groups dedicated to particular fruits. www.nafex.org. On the West Coast, CRFG is another large organization with members in many states and foreign countries, most of them interested in pushing the boundaries of traditional fruit growing and cultivating the unusual and exotic. www.crfg.org. California and northwestern gardeners also can check out an associated forum site at www.cloudforest.com.

Soil and Health Library. Impressive electronic collection of out-of-print books, all available to read online free of charge. www.soil andhealth.org

Sprout People. There are a number of sites providing information on the health benefits of sprouts, and many more that sell sprouting seed. I have listed a few of the latter in the chapter on sprouting. If I were to recommend one resource to learn about how to sprout various kinds of seeds, as well as a very solid source for mail order seeds, it would be the Sprout People website. These folks have been sprouting, and selling their seeds and sprouts to the public, for many years with a sustainable vision. www.sproutpeople.com

Urban Gardening Groups and Community Gardens. There may well be an urban gardening group in your area. Since they have differing names and are only loosely associated with one another, try an Internet search for "urban gardening," or "urban gardeners," plus the name of your city, area, and state. (Try separate searches for each of these locales.) You also could check with your local nursery or university extension agent to see if they know of such a group. Some cities also have community gardens available in which folks may rent gardening spaces. Most of these are operated by local gardening groups. American Community Gardening Association has a searchable list of these at www.communitygarden.org.